Ultimate QuickBooks Bible

The Essential A-Z Handbook for Everyone

Jerry P. G. Bill

TABLE OF CONTENTS

Ultimate QuickBooks Bible

Ultimate QuickBooks Bible

Ultimate QuickBooks Bible

Ultimate QuickBooks Bible

Ultimate QuickBooks Bible

Ultimate QuickBooks Bible

Introduction to QuickBooks

What Is QuickBooks?

QuickBooks is a widely recognized and trusted accounting software designed to simplify financial management for businesses, individuals, and organizations. Created by Intuit, QuickBooks offers tools to help users track income and expenses, manage invoices, monitor cash flow, generate financial reports, and much more. It serves as a digital hub for organizing financial data, enabling users to maintain accurate and efficient records.

QuickBooks is versatile, catering to various industries such as retail, manufacturing, service providers, nonprofits, and more. Whether you're a freelancer, a small business owner, or managing the finances of a larger enterprise, QuickBooks provides the flexibility to meet diverse accounting needs.

The software is available in two main formats:

1. **QuickBooks Desktop**: A locally installed version suitable for users who prefer offline solutions.
2. **QuickBooks Online**: A cloud-based version ideal for those who require remote access and collaboration.

QuickBooks simplifies bookkeeping by automating tasks like transaction categorization, payroll processing, and tax calculations, reducing the chances of human error while saving time.

Key Features and Benefits

Key Features

1. **Invoicing**

   - Create and send professional invoices quickly.
   - Customize templates to match your branding.
   - Automate reminders for overdue payments.

2. **Expense Tracking**

   - Link bank accounts and credit cards to track expenses automatically.
   - Categorize expenses for better organization and reporting.
   - Upload and store digital receipts for easy reference.

3. **Bank Reconciliation**

- o Match bank and credit card transactions with records in QuickBooks.
- o Identify discrepancies and resolve them efficiently.

4. **Financial Reporting**

- o Generate a wide range of reports, including profit and loss, balance sheet, and cash flow statements.
- o Customize reports to highlight specific metrics.

5. **Payroll Management**

- o Calculate employee paychecks, taxes, and deductions.
- o Automate payroll tax filings and compliance tasks.

6. **Inventory Management**

- o Track stock levels in real-time.
- o Set alerts for low inventory.
- o Adjust inventory levels and track costs.

7. Tax Preparation

- Calculate and track sales tax automatically.
- Generate reports for tax filings, minimizing stress during tax season.

8. Integration and Scalability

- Integrate with third-party apps like Shopify, PayPal, and Stripe for enhanced functionality.
- Scale the software's features as your business grows.

Key Benefits

1. Time-Saving Automation

QuickBooks automates repetitive tasks, such as data entry, transaction categorization, and invoice reminders, allowing users to focus on core business activities.

2. **Accuracy in Financial Management**
   By minimizing manual processes,
   QuickBooks reduces the risk of human
   error, ensuring that financial records are
   precise and reliable.

3. **Comprehensive Financial Insights**
   The platform provides real-time insights
   into your financial health, empowering
   informed decision-making.

4. **Ease of Use**
   QuickBooks is user-friendly, offering
   intuitive interfaces and tutorials to help
   beginners navigate its features effortlessly.

5. **Cost-Effectiveness**
   For small and medium-sized businesses,
   QuickBooks provides robust accounting
   tools at a fraction of the cost of hiring an
   accountant.

6. **Accessibility and Flexibility**
   With QuickBooks Online, you can access your financial data anytime, anywhere, and collaborate with your accountant or team members seamlessly.

7. **Compliance Support**
   QuickBooks helps ensure compliance with tax laws and regulations by automating calculations, reminders, and filings.

Choosing the Right Version of QuickBooks for Your Needs

Selecting the right version of QuickBooks depends on your specific requirements, budget, and business size. Below is an overview of the primary QuickBooks options to help you make an informed decision:

QuickBooks Desktop

- **Best For**: Businesses that prefer offline solutions and require advanced inventory and reporting features.
- **Key Variants**:
    - **Pro**: Ideal for small businesses with basic needs.
    - **Premier**: Suited for industry-specific accounting (e.g., nonprofits, contractors).
    - **Enterprise**: Designed for larger businesses with complex accounting needs, offering advanced user permissions and reporting tools.
- **Advantages**: One-time purchase option, robust features, and enhanced control over data.
- **Limitations**: Limited remote access and a steeper learning curve.

QuickBooks Online

- **Best For**: Users who value mobility, collaboration, and real-time access to data.
- **Plans**:

- ○ **Simple Start**: Great for freelancers and sole proprietors.
- ○ **Essentials**: Adds features for managing bills and multiple users.
- ○ **Plus**: Includes inventory tracking and project profitability.
- ○ **Advanced**: Offers advanced analytics and dedicated support.
- **Advantages**: Cloud-based, easy to use, and integrates with various apps.
- **Limitations**: Requires a subscription and relies on internet access.

QuickBooks Self-Employed

- **Best For**: Freelancers and independent contractors managing personal and business finances.
- **Features**: Expense tracking, mileage tracking, and simplified tax preparation.
- **Limitations**: Limited scalability and features compared to other versions.

QuickBooks Mac

- **Best For**: Mac users who prefer desktop software.
- **Features**: Similar to QuickBooks Desktop Pro but optimized for macOS.
- **Limitations**: Less feature-rich than QuickBooks Online or Desktop Enterprise.

Factors to Consider When Choosing a Version

1. **Business Size and Complexity**: Larger businesses may require the advanced features of QuickBooks Enterprise, while sole proprietors can often manage with Simple Start.
2. **Budget**: QuickBooks Online has monthly subscription fees, while QuickBooks Desktop offers a one-time purchase option.
3. **Access Needs**: Choose QuickBooks Online for remote and collaborative

access, or QuickBooks Desktop for offline control.

4. **Industry Requirements**: QuickBooks Premier offers tailored tools for specific industries, such as nonprofits or retail.

5. **Growth Plans**: If you anticipate scaling your business, select a version that can grow with you, like QuickBooks Plus or Enterprise.

Getting Started with QuickBooks

Successfully setting up QuickBooks is the first step to mastering your financial management. This section covers everything you need to get started, from installation to customization, ensuring that your QuickBooks experience is tailored to your needs.

Installing QuickBooks: Step-by-Step Guide

1. Choose Your Version of QuickBooks

Decide whether you want to use QuickBooks Online or QuickBooks Desktop. Your choice will depend on your preference for cloud-based vs. offline use, and your specific business needs.

QuickBooks Online

- Go to the QuickBooks Online website.
- Select the plan that fits your requirements (Simple Start, Essentials, Plus, or Advanced).
- Create an Intuit account or log in with an existing one.
- Follow the prompts to complete your subscription.

QuickBooks Desktop

- Purchase the software from Intuit's website, a trusted retailer, or a licensed distributor.
- Ensure your computer meets the system requirements for the version you've chosen (Pro, Premier, or Enterprise).

2. Download and Install QuickBooks

For QuickBooks Online

- Once you've subscribed, there's no software to download. You'll access your account directly through a web browser.

For QuickBooks Desktop

- **Download the Installer**:
  - Log in to your Intuit account and download the installer file.
  - Save it in a location that's easy to find, such as your desktop or downloads folder.
- **Run the Installer**:
  - Double-click the downloaded file to begin the installation process.
  - Follow the on-screen instructions, choosing your installation type:
    - **Express Install**: Recommended for most users.

- ■ **Custom and Network Options**: For advanced users setting up QuickBooks on multiple computers.
- **Activate QuickBooks**:
  - ○ Once installed, open QuickBooks and enter the license and product numbers from your purchase confirmation email or box.

---

3. Updates and Add-Ons

- **Check for Updates**: Ensure that you have the latest updates by going to Help > Update QuickBooks Desktop.
- **Install Add-Ons**: If needed, you can integrate QuickBooks with other tools or apps, such as payroll or inventory management systems.

Setting Up Your Company File

Your company file is the foundation of your QuickBooks setup. It contains all your financial data, including accounts, transactions, and lists.

1. Start the Setup Wizard

- Open QuickBooks and select **Create a New Company**.
- Use the **Express Start** or **Detailed Start** option based on your preference:
  - **Express Start**: Quick and straightforward, recommended for users with basic needs.
  - **Detailed Start**: Provides more customization during setup, suitable for complex business operations.

---

2. Enter Basic Company Information

- **Business Name**: Enter your company's official name as it should appear on reports and invoices.
- **Industry**: Choose the industry that best matches your business. QuickBooks will

pre-configure accounts based on your selection.

- **Business Type**: Specify your business entity type (e.g., sole proprietorship, partnership, corporation).
- **Fiscal Year Start**: Define when your fiscal year begins.

---

3. Set Up Your Chart of Accounts

- **Use Pre-Configured Options**: QuickBooks offers a suggested list of accounts based on your industry.
- **Add Custom Accounts**: If needed, you can create additional accounts to track specific financial categories.

---

4. Add Key Business Details

- **Customer and Vendor Lists**: Input your existing customers and vendors to streamline transactions.

- **Products and Services**: Add the items you sell, whether they're goods, services, or both.
- **Bank Accounts**: Link your business bank accounts for seamless transaction tracking.

Customizing QuickBooks Preferences

Tailoring QuickBooks preferences ensures that the software aligns with your business operations and makes everyday tasks more efficient.

1. General Settings

- **Navigate to Preferences**: Open the Edit menu in QuickBooks Desktop or the Settings gear icon in QuickBooks Online, and select **Preferences**.
- **Company Settings**: Update basic company information, such as contact

details, business logo, and default email address.

---

2. Financial Preferences

- **Default Accounts**: Assign default accounts for specific tasks (e.g., sales, expenses, payroll).
- **Sales Tax**: Enable and configure sales tax settings if your business is required to collect it.
- **Fiscal Year**: Confirm your fiscal year start date for accurate reporting.

---

3. Invoice and Form Customization

- **Templates**: Choose from pre-designed templates or create a custom one.
- **Branding**: Add your company logo, choose fonts, and set colors to match your branding.

- **Payment Options**: Enable payment links so customers can pay online.

---

4. Notifications and Alerts

- **Reminders**: Set reminders for overdue invoices, upcoming bills, and payroll deadlines.
- **Email Notifications**: Configure email alerts for critical updates, such as low inventory or reconciliation issues.

---

5. Advanced Preferences

- **Multi-Currency**: If you deal with international clients, enable multi-currency settings.
- **User Permissions**: Define user roles and permissions to control who can access specific features.

- **Automation**: Automate recurring invoices, bills, or journal entries to save time.

---

6. Integrations and Add-Ons

- **Apps and Tools**: Explore third-party integrations like PayPal, Shopify, or Stripe to enhance functionality.
- **Payroll Add-On**: If needed, subscribe to QuickBooks Payroll and integrate it into your setup.

---

7. Testing and Adjusting

Once your preferences are configured, test your setup by performing a few mock transactions. Adjust settings as necessary to ensure smooth operations.

Understanding the QuickBooks Interface

QuickBooks is designed to make managing finances straightforward and efficient. Whether you're using QuickBooks Online or QuickBooks Desktop, understanding its interface is essential for navigating the platform effectively and utilizing its powerful features. Let's explore how to master the QuickBooks interface, from basic navigation to pro tips that will save you time and effort.

Navigation Basics

1. QuickBooks Online vs. QuickBooks Desktop

While both versions offer robust tools for financial management, their interfaces differ significantly:

- **QuickBooks Online**: Cloud-based with a modern, web-based design. It's accessible from any device with an internet connection.
- **QuickBooks Desktop**: Installed software with a more traditional interface designed for offline use.

---

2. Logging In

- **QuickBooks Online**:
  - Visit the QuickBooks website and log in using your Intuit account credentials.
  - The home screen serves as your dashboard, providing an overview of your business's financial health.

- **QuickBooks Desktop**:
  - Launch the application on your computer.
  - Open your company file to access the interface.

---

3. Main Navigation Components

The QuickBooks interface is divided into several sections to streamline your workflow:

- **Dashboard/Home Page**:
  - Provides a snapshot of your business's key financial data, such as income, expenses, and profit.
- **Navigation Menu**:
  - In QuickBooks Online, this vertical menu on the left includes links to essential areas like Sales, Expenses, and Reports.
  - In QuickBooks Desktop, the menu bar at the top offers access to Lists,

Customers, Vendors, and
Employees.

- **Search Bar**:
  - ○ Quickly locate transactions, reports,
    or accounts by typing in keywords
    or numbers.
- **Help and Support**:
  - ○ Access Intuit's knowledge base or
    contact support directly from the
    interface.

Key Sections and Features

1. Dashboard Overview

The dashboard is your command center,
summarizing your financial activity:

- **Income and Expense Graph**: Visual
  representation of your cash flow over
  time.
- **Bank Accounts**: Displays balances and
  lets you quickly reconcile transactions.

- **Shortcuts**: Quick access to commonly used actions, like creating an invoice or recording a bill.

---

2. Key Sections

Customers (Sales)

- Manage your customer database, track invoices, and receive payments.
- QuickBooks Online combines these functions under the "Sales" tab, while QuickBooks Desktop separates them into "Customers" and "Invoices."

Vendors (Expenses)

- Track bills, record expenses, and manage vendor relationships.
- Create recurring expense templates for efficiency.

Banking

- Link your bank and credit card accounts for automatic transaction imports.
- Use the bank feed to categorize and match transactions with minimal effort.

Reports

- Generate financial statements, such as profit and loss reports, balance sheets, and cash flow statements.
- Customize reports to focus on specific timeframes or data points.

Taxes

- Set up sales tax rates and manage tax liabilities.
- QuickBooks can calculate and track sales tax automatically based on your settings.

---

3. Special Features

- **Projects**: Track income and expenses for specific projects to measure profitability (available in QuickBooks Online Plus and Advanced).

- **Payroll**: Manage employee wages, deductions, and tax filings.
- **Inventory**: Track stock levels and costs, reorder items, and manage product sales.

Tips and Tricks for Efficient Navigation

1. Keyboard Shortcuts

- **QuickBooks Desktop**:
  - Ctrl + I: Create Invoice.
  - Ctrl + W: Write Check.
  - Ctrl + R: Open Register.
- **QuickBooks Online**:
  - Use global search (/) to quickly locate anything.
  - Access shortcuts like creating a new transaction (+ New button) from anywhere.

---

2. Customize Your Interface

- **QuickBooks Online**: Rearrange dashboard widgets and add shortcuts to frequently used functions.
- **QuickBooks Desktop**: Modify your home page by enabling/disabling modules to suit your workflow.

---

3. Use the Search Function

- Leverage the search bar to locate transactions or reports instantly, saving time compared to manual browsing.

---

4. Automate Tasks

- Set up recurring invoices, bills, or journal entries to reduce repetitive data entry.
- Automate bank feeds to streamline transaction categorization.

---

5. Explore the Help Menu

- Access video tutorials, step-by-step guides, and troubleshooting tips directly from the Help menu.

---

6. Multitasking in QuickBooks Online

- Open multiple tabs in your browser to work on different sections simultaneously, such as viewing reports while creating invoices.

---

7. Save Frequently Used Reports

- Mark your most-used reports as favorites for quick access.
- Schedule reports to be sent automatically via email.

---

8. Take Advantage of Training Resources

- Use Intuit's training tools or community forums to deepen your understanding of advanced features.

Managing Accounts and Lists

Managing accounts and lists in QuickBooks is the foundation of effective financial management. By organizing your Chart of Accounts, maintaining accurate customer, vendor, and employee records, and leveraging the Products and Services list, you ensure your business runs smoothly and your financial data stays accurate.

Chart of Accounts: Creating and Managing Accounts

The **Chart of Accounts** is the backbone of your accounting system in QuickBooks. It categorizes all your financial transactions, helping you track income, expenses, assets, liabilities, and equity.

1. What Is the Chart of Accounts?

The Chart of Accounts is a list of all the accounts your business uses to record transactions. Each account falls into a specific category:

- **Assets**: Cash, bank accounts, receivables, and inventory.
- **Liabilities**: Loans, credit card balances, and accounts payable.
- **Income**: Revenue from sales or services.
- **Expenses**: Costs incurred in operating your business.
- **Equity**: Owner's investments, retained earnings, and net income.

---

2. Creating Accounts

To add an account in QuickBooks:

- **QuickBooks Online**:
  1. Go to **Settings** > **Chart of Accounts**.
  2. Click **New**.
  3. Choose the account type (e.g., Expense, Income).
  4. Select a detail type (e.g., Utilities for Expense).
  5. Name the account and add a description if needed.
  6. Save.
- **QuickBooks Desktop**:
  1. Navigate to **Lists** > **Chart of Accounts**.
  2. Click **Account** > **New**.
  3. Select the account type and fill in the details.
  4. Save and close.

---

3. Managing Accounts

- **Editing Accounts**: Adjust account details, such as names or descriptions, as your business evolves.
- **Merging Accounts**: Combine duplicate accounts to streamline reporting (available in QuickBooks Desktop).
- **Deleting/Deactivating Accounts**: Hide unused accounts to keep your Chart of Accounts clean. QuickBooks retains historical data for deactivated accounts.

---

4. Best Practices

- Avoid creating too many accounts to keep the Chart of Accounts manageable.
- Regularly review accounts for accuracy and eliminate duplicates.
- Use sub-accounts for detailed tracking within broader categories (e.g., "Office Supplies" under "Expenses").

Managing Customers, Vendors, and Employees

Efficiently tracking customers, vendors, and employees in QuickBooks helps you manage relationships, payments, and payroll effectively.

1. Customers

Customers are the lifeblood of any business, and QuickBooks makes it easy to manage them.

- **Adding a New Customer**:
    - **QuickBooks Online**: Go to **Sales** > **Customers** > **New Customer**.
    - **QuickBooks Desktop**: Navigate to **Customers** > **Customer Center** > **New Customer & Job**.
    - Fill in details like name, email, billing address, and payment terms.
- **Tracking Customer Activity**:
    - View transaction histories, outstanding invoices, and payment records.
- **Invoicing and Payments**:

- ○ Quickly create invoices, apply payments, and send reminders for overdue balances.
- **Customer Groups**:
  - ○ Organize customers by categories such as "VIP Clients" or "Frequent Buyers."

---

2. Vendors

Vendors supply your business with goods or services. Keeping accurate vendor records ensures smooth transactions.

- **Adding a New Vendor**:
  - ○ **QuickBooks Online**: Go to **Expenses > Vendors > New Vendor**.
  - ○ **QuickBooks Desktop**: Navigate to **Vendors > Vendor Center > New Vendor**.
  - ○ Enter details such as name, tax ID, and payment terms.

- **Tracking Vendor Bills and Payments**:
  - Record bills, track due dates, and schedule payments to maintain good relationships.
- **Vendor Reports**:
  - Generate reports like Vendor Balance Summary to monitor outstanding liabilities.

---

3. Employees

QuickBooks supports payroll processing, making employee management seamless.

- **Adding Employees**:
  - Enter personal details, tax information, and salary details.
  - **QuickBooks Online**: Go to **Payroll > Employees > Add Employee**.
  - **QuickBooks Desktop**: Navigate to **Employees > Employee Center > New Employee.**
- **Processing Payroll**:

- ○ Calculate wages, deduct taxes, and issue paychecks.
- **Tracking Time**:
  - ○ Use time-tracking features to monitor hours worked.

Utilizing Products and Services Lists

The Products and Services list in QuickBooks helps you track what your business sells, whether it's goods, services, or a mix of both.

1. Setting Up Products and Services

To create a new item:

- **QuickBooks Online**:
  1. Go to **Sales** > **Products and Services** > **New.**
  2. Choose the item type (Non-inventory, Inventory, or Service).
  3. Enter details such as name, SKU, price, and sales tax status.

- **QuickBooks Desktop**:
  1. Navigate to **Lists** > **Item List** > **New Item.**
  2. Select the type (Inventory, Non-inventory, or Service) and fill in the required fields.

---

2. Tracking Inventory

- QuickBooks automatically adjusts inventory levels based on purchases and sales.
- Set up reorder points to get alerts when stock runs low.

---

3. Managing Services

- For service-based businesses, track hours billed and rates charged for different services.
- Use timesheets or integrate with time-tracking tools for precise invoicing.

---

4. Generating Reports

- Use the Products/Services list to analyze sales trends, identify top-selling items, and evaluate profitability.
- Reports include "Sales by Product/Service Summary" and "Inventory Valuation Summary."

---

5. Organizing the List

- Group similar items into categories for better organization (e.g., "Office Supplies," "Consulting Services").
- Mark inactive items you no longer sell to keep your list clutter-free.

Best Practices for Managing Accounts and Lists

1. **Consistency is Key**: Use uniform naming conventions for accounts, customers, vendors, and products.
2. **Regular Reviews**: Periodically review and clean up lists to eliminate duplicates or inactive entries.
3. **Leverage Automation**: Automate recurring entries and inventory tracking to save time.
4. **Integrate with Other Tools**: Sync with CRM software or inventory management tools for added efficiency.
5. **Use Reports**: Generate and analyze reports to gain insights into your financial data and operations.

Recording Transactions

Recording transactions is the cornerstone of effective financial management in QuickBooks. By accurately creating invoices, recording payments, handling sales receipts, and managing refunds or credit memos, you ensure your financial records remain precise and organized. Below, we'll explore how to handle these tasks extensively.

Creating and Sending Invoices

Invoices are essential for requesting payment from customers. QuickBooks makes it simple to create and send professional invoices tailored to your business needs.

1. Creating an Invoice

QuickBooks Online:

1. Navigate to **Sales > Invoices > New Invoice.**
2. Select a **customer** from the dropdown list or add a new one.
3. Enter the **invoice date** and **due date**.
4. Add **products or services** to the invoice. If the item isn't listed, you can create it on the spot.
5. Include the **quantity**, **rate**, and **tax details**, if applicable. QuickBooks automatically calculates the total.
6. Customize the invoice with additional notes or terms (e.g., "Payment due in 30 days").
7. Save and preview the invoice to check its accuracy.

QuickBooks Desktop:

1. Go to **Customers** > **Create Invoices** from the main menu.
2. Select a template that matches your branding.
3. Add the customer's details and fill in the invoice information.
4. List the items or services and verify the totals.
5. Save the invoice or print/email it directly to the customer.

---

2. Sending Invoices

- **Emailing Invoices**: QuickBooks allows direct emailing.

  - Review the email template and personalize it as needed.
  - Attach supporting documents (e.g., contracts or estimates).
- **Printing and Mailing**: For customers who prefer paper invoices, QuickBooks

supports batch printing for bulk mailings.

- **Tracking Invoices**:

    - Use the **Invoices tab** to monitor outstanding balances.
    - Set up **automated reminders** for overdue payments.

Recording Payments and Sales Receipts

Recording payments and sales receipts in QuickBooks ensures your revenue is accounted for accurately and reconciles with your bank deposits.

1. Recording Customer Payments

When a customer pays an invoice, QuickBooks helps you apply the payment to the correct account and invoice.

QuickBooks Online:

1. Go to + **New** > **Receive Payment.**
2. Select the customer and the invoice being paid.
3. Enter the payment details:
   - Payment **date**.
   - Payment **method** (e.g., check, cash, credit card).
   - Deposit **to** (bank account).
4. Verify the payment amount.
5. Save and close.

QuickBooks Desktop:

1. Navigate to **Customers** > **Receive Payments.**
2. Choose the customer from the dropdown menu.
3. Select the invoice(s) to apply the payment to.
4. Enter payment information and deposit location.
5. Save.

2. Recording Sales Receipts

Sales receipts are used when payment is received at the time of sale.

QuickBooks Online:

1. Go to + **New** > **Sales Receipt.**
2. Choose the customer and payment method.
3. Add items or services sold, quantity, and rate.
4. Confirm the total amount and sales tax.
5. Save and email or print the receipt.

QuickBooks Desktop:

1. Go to **Customers** > **Enter Sales Receipts.**
2. Fill in the customer details and payment information.
3. Add the items or services.
4. Save and print/email the receipt.

3. Depositing Payments

If you don't deposit payments immediately, record them in **Undeposited Funds** first. When ready to deposit:

- **QuickBooks Online**: Go to + **New** > **Bank Deposit**, select payments, and deposit them into your bank account.
- **QuickBooks Desktop**: Navigate to **Banking** > **Make Deposits**, select payments, and complete the deposit.

Handling Refunds and Credit Memos

Refunds and credit memos address situations where you need to return money or credit to a customer.

1. Creating a Refund

Refunds occur when you return money directly to the customer.

QuickBooks Online:

1. Go to + **New** > **Refund Receipt.**
2. Select the customer and payment method.
3. Add the refunded item/service, quantity, and refund amount.
4. Choose the bank account or payment method used for the refund.
5. Save and send the receipt to the customer.

QuickBooks Desktop:

1. Navigate to **Customers** > **Create Credit Memos/Refunds.**
2. Enter the customer details and refunded items/services.
3. Issue the refund as cash, check, or credit card.

---

2. Creating a Credit Memo

Credit memos allow you to apply credit to a customer's future invoices.

QuickBooks Online:

1. Go to **+ New** > **Credit Memo.**
2. Select the customer and enter the items or services being credited.
3. Save the credit memo. It will appear as available credit in the customer's account.

QuickBooks Desktop:

1. Go to **Customers** > **Create Credit Memos/Refunds.**
2. Add the credited items or services.
3. Save and choose how to apply the credit:
    - Retain for future invoices.
    - Refund the customer directly.

---

3. Applying Credits

Credits can be applied to outstanding invoices or used as a payment:

- **QuickBooks Online**: Open the invoice, select the available credit, and apply it.

- **QuickBooks Desktop**: Use the **Receive Payments** window to apply credit to the customer's balance.

Tips for Efficient Transaction Recording

1. **Set Up Automation**: Use recurring invoices and reminders for overdue payments to save time.
2. **Reconcile Regularly**: Match recorded transactions with bank statements to ensure accuracy.
3. **Double-Check Customer and Payment Details**: Avoid errors by verifying details before saving transactions.
4. **Track Refunds and Credits**: Keep an eye on refunded amounts and ensure they're accurately reflected in reports.
5. **Use Tags or Classes**: Categorize transactions for better financial analysis.

Banking and Reconciliation

Efficiently managing your banking in QuickBooks is vital for maintaining accurate financial records. QuickBooks provides tools to link bank accounts, record deposits and transfers, and reconcile bank statements, ensuring your accounts are balanced and up-to-date.

Linking Bank Accounts

Connecting your bank accounts to QuickBooks streamlines transaction management and reduces manual data entry.

Benefits of Linking Bank Accounts

- **Automatic Transaction Import**: Your bank transactions are automatically pulled into QuickBooks, saving time.
- **Real-Time Updates**: View your latest bank activity directly within QuickBooks.
- **Easier Reconciliation**: Match imported transactions with your QuickBooks records quickly.

---

1. Linking a Bank Account in QuickBooks Online

1. **Navigate to the Banking Tab**:

    ○ Go to **Banking** or **Transactions** > **Banking**.
2. **Select Connect Account**:

    ○ If this is your first connection, click **Connect Account**.

  ○ For additional accounts, click **Link Account** at the top right.

3. **Search for Your Bank**:

  ○ Use the search bar to locate your bank. QuickBooks supports connections with most financial institutions.

4. **Log In to Your Bank Account**:

  ○ Enter your online banking credentials securely.
  ○ Follow the on-screen prompts to grant QuickBooks access to your account.

5. **Choose Accounts to Link**:

  ○ Select the specific account (e.g., checking, savings, or credit card) you want to connect.
  ○ Assign it to the appropriate QuickBooks account (e.g., Checking, Savings).

6. **Import Transactions**:

   o Choose the date range for imported transactions (e.g., the last 90 days).
   o QuickBooks will begin importing transactions.

---

2. Linking a Bank Account in QuickBooks Desktop

1. **Open the Bank Feeds Center**:

   o Go to **Banking > Bank Feeds > Set Up Bank Feed for an Account.**

2. **Find Your Bank**:

   o Search for your bank from the list of supported institutions.

3. **Log In to Your Online Banking**:

   o Enter your online banking credentials.

4. **Match to Your QuickBooks Account**:

   o Select the QuickBooks account that
   corresponds to the bank account.
5. **Download Transactions**:

   o Once connected, download recent
   transactions for review and
   categorization.

Recording Deposits and Transfers

Deposits and transfers are critical financial
activities, and recording them accurately ensures
proper account management.

---

1. Recording Deposits

Deposits reflect incoming money, such as
payments from customers, loans, or other
sources.

QuickBooks Online:

1. **Go to Bank Deposit**:

   o Select + **New** > **Bank Deposit.**

2. **Choose an Account**:

   o Select the bank account where the deposit was made.

3. **Enter Deposit Details**:

   o Select payments received that need to be deposited.
   o Add other amounts, if any (e.g., loan proceeds, owner contributions).

4. **Review and Save**:

   o Double-check the details and save the deposit.

QuickBooks Desktop:

1. **Navigate to Make Deposits**:

- Go to **Banking > Make Deposits.**
2. **Select Payments**:

- Choose payments waiting to be deposited from the **Undeposited Funds** window.
3. **Enter Deposit Information**:

- Specify the deposit account, date, and additional deposit items.
4. **Save and Print**:

- Save the deposit and print a deposit slip if needed.

---

2. Recording Transfers

Transfers involve moving funds between two accounts (e.g., from checking to savings).

QuickBooks Online:

1. **Go to Transfer**:

- Select + **New** > **Transfer.**
2. **Enter Transfer Details**:

  - Specify the **transfer from** and **transfer to** accounts.
  - Input the **amount** and **date**.
3. **Save and Close**:

  - Confirm the information and save.

QuickBooks Desktop:

1. **Navigate to Transfer Funds**:

  - Go to **Banking** > **Transfer Funds.**
2. **Fill in the Transfer Details**:

  - Choose the source and destination accounts.
  - Enter the amount and date.
3. **Save**:

  - Save the transfer to update your records.

Reconciling Bank Statements

Bank reconciliation is the process of matching your QuickBooks records with your bank statements. This ensures that all transactions are accounted for and errors are identified.

Why Reconciliation Is Important

- Identifies missing or duplicate transactions.
- Ensures your financial records are accurate for reporting and tax purposes.
- Detects unauthorized transactions or fraud.

Steps to Reconcile Bank Statements

QuickBooks Online:

1. **Access Reconciliation**:

   ○ Go to **Accounting** > **Reconcile.**
2. **Select the Account**:

   ○ Choose the bank or credit card
   account to reconcile.
3. **Enter Statement Information**:

   ○ Input the **statement ending
   balance** and **ending date** from your
   bank statement.
4. **Match Transactions**:

   ○ Review transactions in QuickBooks
   and check them off as they appear
   on your statement.
5. **Resolve Discrepancies**:

   ○ Adjust for missing transactions or
   errors.
   ○ Use QuickBooks' tools to find and
   fix differences.

6. **Finish Reconciliation**:

   ○ Once all transactions match,
     confirm reconciliation.

QuickBooks Desktop:

1. **Open Reconciliation**:

   ○ Go to **Banking > Reconcile.**
2. **Enter Statement Details**:

   ○ Provide the **statement date** and
     ending balance.
3. **Mark Cleared Transactions**:

   ○ Check off transactions that match
     your statement.
4. **Identify Discrepancies**:

   ○ QuickBooks highlights
     unreconciled amounts.

o   Add missing transactions or correct errors.

5. **Complete Reconciliation**:

o   Reconcile the account and generate reconciliation reports.

Tips for Successful Reconciliation

1. **Reconcile Monthly**: Regular reconciliation makes the process faster and easier.
2. **Use Filters**: Filter transactions by type, date, or amount to find discrepancies quickly.
3. **Verify Opening Balances**: Ensure your QuickBooks opening balance matches the bank's opening balance.
4. **Investigate Differences**: Look for duplicate entries, missed transactions, or incorrect categorizations.
5. **Review Reports**: After reconciliation, review reconciliation reports for accuracy.

Streamlining Banking and Reconciliation

QuickBooks simplifies banking and
reconciliation with tools like automatic
transaction matching, categorization rules, and
integration with major banks. By linking
accounts, recording deposits and transfers
accurately, and reconciling bank statements
regularly, you'll maintain accurate, audit-ready
financial records. These practices not only save
time but also enhance your confidence in
managing your business finances.

Managing Expenses and Bills

Effective expense and bill management is a cornerstone of accurate financial tracking. QuickBooks provides tools to manage all aspects of expense tracking, from entering and paying bills to monitoring recurring expenses and handling vendor credits. This functionality ensures that your cash flow remains healthy and that your vendor relationships are professionally managed.

Entering and Paying Bills

QuickBooks makes it simple to enter and pay bills, ensuring that all outstanding liabilities are recorded and paid on time.

1. Entering Bills

Entering bills in QuickBooks creates a record of the money you owe vendors or suppliers for goods and services received.

QuickBooks Online:

1. **Navigate to Enter Bills**:

   - Go to + **New** > **Bill** under the **Vendors** section.
2. **Select the Vendor**:

   - Choose the vendor you received the bill from.
   - If the vendor is new, you can quickly add them by clicking **Add New**.
3. **Enter Bill Details**:

- o **Bill Date**: Enter the date on the invoice.
- o **Due Date**: Specify the payment due date to ensure timely payment tracking.
- o **Category or Item Details**: Categorize the expense or select the purchased item from your products and services list.
- o **Amount**: Enter the total amount of the bill, including tax if applicable.

4. **Attach Supporting Documents** (Optional):

- o Upload the invoice or receipt for future reference.

5. **Save and Close**:

- o Save the bill to record the liability.

QuickBooks Desktop:

1. **Navigate to Enter Bills**:

- o Go to **Vendors** > **Enter Bills**.

2. **Fill in Vendor and Bill Information**:

   ○ Select the vendor and enter the invoice date, amount, and due date.

3. **Categorize the Expense**:

   ○ Choose the expense account or item linked to the purchase.

4. **Save**:

   ○ Click **Save & Close** to finish.

---

2. Paying Bills

Once a bill is entered, QuickBooks allows you to pay it efficiently, ensuring timely vendor payments.

QuickBooks Online:

1. **Go to Pay Bills**:

   ○ Navigate to + **New** > **Pay Bills**.

2. **Select the Account**:

   ○ Choose the bank or credit card
     account used for payment.
3. **Choose Bills to Pay**:

   ○ Select the bills you want to pay.
4. **Enter Payment Details**:

   ○ Specify the payment date and
     method (e.g., check, electronic
     payment).
5. **Save and Close**:

   ○ Record the payment and update the
     vendor's balance.

QuickBooks Desktop:

1. **Navigate to Pay Bills**:

   ○ Go to **Vendors** > **Pay Bills**.
2. **Select Bills for Payment**:

    o Check the box next to the bills you want to pay.

3. **Enter Payment Information**:

    o Choose the payment account and method.

4. **Print Checks** (Optional):

    o If paying by check, you can print them directly from QuickBooks.

5. **Save**:

    o Confirm the payment and update the vendor record.

Tracking Recurring Expenses

Recurring expenses are regular payments for utilities, subscriptions, or rent. Automating these transactions in QuickBooks saves time and ensures you don't miss any payments.

Setting Up Recurring Expenses

QuickBooks Online:

1. **Go to Recurring Transactions**:

   o Navigate to **Settings** > **Recurring Transactions**.

2. **Create a New Template**:

   o Click **New** and select the transaction type, such as a bill or expense.

3. **Enter Recurrence Details**:

   o Choose a name for the template and set the schedule (e.g., weekly, monthly).
   o Specify the vendor, category, and amount.

4. **Save Template**:

   o Once saved, QuickBooks automatically generates transactions based on the set schedule.

QuickBooks Desktop:

1. **Open Memorized Transactions List**:

   ○ Go to **Lists** > **Memorized Transaction List**.
2. **Create a Memorized Transaction**:

   ○ Enter the expense or bill you want to recur and click **Memorize** at the top.
3. **Set Schedule**:

   ○ Choose how often QuickBooks should remind you or enter the transaction automatically.
4. **Save**:

   ○ Save the template for future use.

Managing Recurring Expenses

- **Edit Templates**: Update recurring expense templates as needed (e.g., changes in amount or frequency).
- **Monitor Upcoming Payments**: Review scheduled expenses to ensure they match your budget.
- **Pause or Delete Templates**: Temporarily disable or delete templates when no longer needed.

Managing Vendor Credits

Vendor credits represent refunds or adjustments for overpayments, returned goods, or discounts. QuickBooks helps you record and apply these credits efficiently.

Recording Vendor Credits

QuickBooks Online:

1. **Enter Vendor Credit**:

   ○ Go to + **New** > **Vendor Credit**.
2. **Select the Vendor**:

   ○ Choose the vendor providing the credit.
3. **Enter Credit Details**:

   ○ Specify the items or expenses being credited and the amounts.
4. **Save and Close**:

   ○ Record the credit for future application.

QuickBooks Desktop:

1. **Navigate to Vendor Credit**:

   ○ Go to **Vendors** > **Enter Bills** > **Credit** option at the top.
2. **Enter Details**:

- o Select the vendor and enter the credit amount and reason.
3. **Save:**

  - o Record the credit.

Applying Vendor Credits

QuickBooks Online:

1. **Pay Bills:**

   - o When paying bills, select the bill and apply the credit to reduce the amount owed.
2. **Confirm Application:**

   - o QuickBooks automatically adjusts the payment total.

QuickBooks Desktop:

1. **Apply Credits:**

- ○ When paying bills, click **Set Credits** to view available credits.

2. **Select Credit**:

- ○ Apply the desired credit to the bill and adjust the payment amount.

3. **Save**:

- ○ Record the payment and credit application.

Best Practices for Managing Expenses and Bills

1. **Stay Organized**: Regularly update vendor details and categorize expenses accurately.
2. **Use Automation**: Set up recurring expenses to reduce manual entry.
3. **Reconcile Vendor Accounts**: Periodically review vendor balances to identify discrepancies.

4. **Track Due Dates**: Use QuickBooks' reminders and reporting tools to avoid late payments.
5. **Leverage Reports**: Run expense and vendor reports to gain insights into your spending patterns.

Payroll Management in QuickBooks

Managing payroll is a critical task for any business that employs staff. QuickBooks simplifies payroll management by integrating tools to set up payroll, process paychecks, and handle taxes and deductions efficiently. This section covers the essentials of payroll management, ensuring compliance and accurate record-keeping.

Setting Up Payroll in QuickBooks

The payroll setup process is vital for ensuring accurate employee payments and tax compliance.

1. QuickBooks Payroll Plans

QuickBooks offers different payroll plans, including Core, Premium, and Elite for QuickBooks Online, or Enhanced and Assisted Payroll for QuickBooks Desktop. Each plan includes varying features such as automated tax filing, direct deposit, and advanced HR support.

---

2. Setting Up Payroll in QuickBooks Online

1. **Access Payroll Settings**:

   o Navigate to **Payroll** in the left menu and click **Get Started**.
2. **Add Your Business Information**:

   o Provide your Employer Identification Number (EIN), business type, and address.

○ Verify your state and federal tax accounts are active.

3. **Enter Employee Information**:

○ Add employee details, including names, addresses, Social Security numbers, and pay rates.
○ Specify employment type (full-time, part-time, or contractor) and payment frequency (e.g., weekly, bi-weekly).

4. **Set Up Pay Types**:

○ Choose the types of pay applicable, such as hourly, salary, bonuses, or overtime.

5. **Enter Tax Details**:

○ Input federal, state, and local tax information for each employee. QuickBooks uses this data to calculate withholding amounts.

6. **Choose Payment Methods**:

- Set up direct deposit or paper checks based on employee preferences.

7. **Complete Tax Forms**:

- Provide tax forms like W-4 for employees and ensure you've filed employer forms such as 941, 940, or state-specific filings.

8. **Review and Save**:

- Double-check all details and complete the payroll setup.

---

3. Setting Up Payroll in QuickBooks Desktop

1. **Activate Payroll**:

- Go to **Employees** > **Payroll Setup**.
- Choose your payroll service plan (Basic, Enhanced, or Assisted).

2. **Enter Company and Employee Information**:

   ○ Add your business details and employee information, similar to QuickBooks Online.

3. **Set Up Payroll Items**:

   ○ Define earnings, deductions, and tax types.
   ○ Create custom payroll items for unique scenarios like health insurance or 401(k) contributions.

4. **Establish Payment Preferences**:

   ○ Set up direct deposit if applicable or print checks directly from QuickBooks.

Processing Employee Paychecks

After setting up payroll, QuickBooks streamlines the paycheck processing workflow to ensure timely and accurate payments.

1. Running Payroll

QuickBooks Online:

1. **Access Payroll Center**:

   o Go to **Payroll** > **Employees**.
2. **Start Payroll**:

   o Click **Run Payroll** and select the pay period.
3. **Verify Employee Hours**:

   o Enter or confirm hours worked, including overtime or bonuses.
4. **Review Payroll**:

   o Check gross pay, deductions, and net pay.
   o Adjust any details if necessary.

5. **Submit Payroll**:

   o Confirm and submit the payroll.
   o QuickBooks processes direct deposits or prepares paychecks for printing.

QuickBooks Desktop:

1. **Navigate to Payroll Center**:

   o Go to **Employees** > **Pay Employees**.
2. **Select Employees and Pay Period**:

   o Choose the employees being paid and the date range.
3. **Enter Hours and Adjustments**:

   o Input regular hours, overtime, and any other pay adjustments.
4. **Create Paychecks**:

   o Review details and create checks or process direct deposits.

2. Issuing Paychecks

1. Direct Deposit:

- QuickBooks transmits employee payments directly to their bank accounts.
- Employees receive pay stubs with detailed breakdowns of their earnings and deductions.

2. Printed Checks:

- Use compatible QuickBooks check stock to print physical checks.

3. Tracking and Reporting Payroll

- Use QuickBooks payroll reports to monitor total wages, tax withholdings, and deductions.

- Generate year-to-date summaries for employees and ensure accurate W-2 or 1099 filings.

Handling Payroll Taxes and Deductions

Payroll taxes and deductions are essential for compliance with federal, state, and local laws. QuickBooks simplifies the calculation, tracking, and remittance of taxes.

---

1. Tax Calculation

QuickBooks automatically calculates payroll taxes based on employee details and your business's location. Taxes include:

- **Federal Taxes**: Social Security, Medicare, and federal income tax.
- **State Taxes**: State income tax, unemployment insurance, or disability insurance, if applicable.

- **Local Taxes**: City, county, or municipality taxes.

---

2. Setting Up Deductions

1. Employee Benefits:

- Add deductions for benefits such as health insurance, retirement contributions (e.g., 401(k)), or garnishments.

2. Custom Deductions:

- Create deductions unique to your organization, such as union fees or charitable contributions.

3. Post-Tax and Pre-Tax Deductions:

- Specify whether deductions should be taken before or after taxes.

---

3. Tax Filings

Automated Filings:

- QuickBooks Online Payroll (Premium and Elite plans) automatically files federal and state payroll taxes.
- Assisted Payroll in QuickBooks Desktop handles tax filings for you.

Manual Filings:

- Basic payroll plans require manual filing of tax forms. Use QuickBooks reports to extract necessary data.

---

4. Tax Payments

1. **Electronic Payments**:

   ○ QuickBooks enables electronic filing and payment of payroll taxes to the IRS and state agencies.

2. **Manual Payments**:

- Generate payment vouchers and remit taxes via check or direct deposit.

---

5. Year-End Payroll Tasks

1. Generate Tax Forms:

- Prepare and distribute W-2s for employees and 1099s for contractors.
- File employer forms like 940 (annual FUTA tax return).

2. Reconcile Payroll Accounts:

- Match payroll reports with your general ledger to ensure accuracy.

3. Archive Payroll Data:

- Retain payroll records for tax and compliance purposes.

Best Practices for Payroll Management

1. **Double-Check Entries**: Always verify employee information, hours, and tax details before processing payroll.
2. **Stay Compliant**: Regularly update tax tables and ensure adherence to federal, state, and local regulations.
3. **Leverage Automation**: Use recurring payroll schedules and automated tax payments to save time.
4. **Review Reports**: Analyze payroll reports to track expenses, monitor trends, and identify potential errors.
5. **Keep Records Secure**: Safeguard payroll records to protect employee privacy and meet compliance standards.

Tracking Taxes in QuickBooks

Effective tax management is crucial for any business to maintain compliance with government regulations and ensure smooth financial operations. QuickBooks provides powerful tools to help businesses set up tax rates, collect and record sales tax, and generate accurate tax reports.

Setting Up Sales Tax Rates

Setting up sales tax correctly is the first step in tax tracking, especially for businesses that deal with taxable goods or services.

1. Understanding Sales Tax Basics

Sales tax is a government-imposed charge applied to the sale of goods and services. The rate and rules vary by state, county, or city, so understanding your local regulations is essential.

2. Setting Up Sales Tax in QuickBooks Online

1. **Navigate to Sales Tax Settings**:

   - Go to **Taxes** in the left-hand menu.
2. **Add Your Tax Agency**:

   - Click **Set up sales tax** and add the agency responsible for collecting taxes (e.g., state tax agency).
3. **Set Up Tax Rates**:

   - QuickBooks Online can automatically calculate sales tax rates based on your business location and customer shipping addresses.

o For manual setup, select **Custom Rate** and input the required tax percentage.

4. **Link Tax Rates to Customers and Products**:

o Assign tax rates to specific customers or sales items to ensure accurate calculations during transactions.

---

3. Setting Up Sales Tax in QuickBooks Desktop

1. **Access the Sales Tax Center**:

o Go to **Edit** > **Preferences** > **Sales Tax** > **Company Preferences**.

2. **Enable Sales Tax**:

o Check **Yes, my company charges sales tax** to activate tax tracking.

3. **Add Tax Agencies**:

   ○ Click **Add Sales Tax Item** and
      input details for your tax agency,
      such as name, description, and tax
      rate.
4. **Define Taxable Items**:

   ○ Mark products and services as
      taxable in your item list to ensure
      QuickBooks applies sales tax
      automatically.

---

4. Handling Multiple Tax Rates

Businesses operating in multiple jurisdictions
may need to manage different sales tax rates.
QuickBooks supports the addition of multiple
tax rates and allows you to set a default rate for
specific regions.

Collecting and Recording Sales Tax

Once sales tax rates are set up, collecting and recording tax during transactions becomes seamless.

1. Invoicing Customers with Sales Tax

When creating invoices or sales receipts, QuickBooks automatically calculates and applies sales tax based on the customer's location and the taxable items in the transaction.

Steps in QuickBooks Online:

1. Create an invoice or sales receipt.
2. Add taxable products or services.
3. QuickBooks will calculate the tax amount based on the customer's shipping address and applicable rates.

Steps in QuickBooks Desktop:

1. Open the **Create Invoices** window.
2. Select the customer and add items.

3. QuickBooks applies the appropriate sales tax rate based on the customer's profile.

---

2. Tracking Tax-Exempt Sales

Some customers or items may be tax-exempt (e.g., non-profit organizations or wholesale transactions).

- **Mark Customers as Tax-Exempt**:

  - In the customer profile, check the tax-exempt option and specify the exemption reason.
- **Exclude Tax on Certain Items**:

  - In the product/service list, mark items as non-taxable if they qualify for exemptions.

---

3. Recording Sales Tax Payments

Once sales tax is collected, it needs to be recorded and eventually paid to the tax agency.

Steps in QuickBooks Online:

1. Go to **Taxes** > **Sales Tax**.
2. Click **Record Tax Payment** and select the tax agency.
3. Enter the payment amount and date.

Steps in QuickBooks Desktop:

1. Navigate to **Vendors** > **Sales Tax** > **Pay Sales Tax**.
2. Select the tax agency and tax period.
3. Confirm the amount and process the payment.

Generating Tax Reports

Tax reports are essential for monitoring collected taxes and preparing for tax filings. QuickBooks provides detailed and customizable tax reports to help businesses stay organized.

1. Common Tax Reports in QuickBooks

- **Sales Tax Liability Report**:
  - Displays the total sales tax collected, owed, and payable to tax agencies.
- **Taxable Sales Summary**:
  - Summarizes all taxable and non-taxable sales within a specific period.
- **Sales Tax Revenue Report**:
  - Breaks down collected sales tax by customer or transaction.

---

2. Generating Reports in QuickBooks Online

1. Go to **Reports** in the left menu.
2. Search for **Sales Tax Liability** or other tax reports.
3. Customize the date range and filters as needed.
4. Review the report and export it if necessary.

3. Generating Reports in QuickBooks Desktop

1. Navigate to **Reports** > **Vendors & Payables** > **Sales Tax Liability**.
2. Set the date range for the reporting period.
3. View, print, or export the report for your records.

4. Using Tax Reports for Filing

QuickBooks tax reports provide all the details needed to complete state and federal tax forms. Use the following process to streamline filings:

1. Review the Sales Tax Liability report for accuracy.
2. Confirm payments against recorded transactions.
3. Submit tax returns electronically through QuickBooks (if supported) or manually using the report details.

Best Practices for Tracking Taxes in QuickBooks

1. **Keep Rates Up to Date**: Regularly review tax rates for changes and update them in QuickBooks.
2. **Audit Taxable Items**: Periodically check your product and service lists to ensure proper tax settings.
3. **Reconcile Tax Accounts**: Reconcile sales tax collected with your bank statements to avoid discrepancies.
4. **Monitor Deadlines**: Stay on top of tax filing and payment deadlines to avoid penalties.
5. **Leverage Automation**: Use QuickBooks features like auto-calculate taxes and scheduled reports to simplify tax tracking.

Generating Reports in QuickBooks

Generating reports is one of the most powerful features of QuickBooks, providing critical insights into the financial health of a business. From understanding cash flow to tracking profitability, reports allow business owners, managers, and accountants to make informed decisions. QuickBooks offers an extensive set of reports that can be customized, exported, and shared. This section will cover the essential financial reports, how to customize reports for specific business needs, and how to export and share these reports for various purposes.

Essential Financial Reports

QuickBooks offers a wide range of reports, each serving different aspects of financial management. Below are the essential financial reports every business should be familiar with:

1. Profit and Loss (Income Statement)

The Profit and Loss report is one of the most important financial documents, showing the company's revenues, expenses, and net profit or loss over a specific period.

- **Purpose**: It helps business owners understand how much they are earning versus spending. It provides a summary of revenue and expenses, showing whether the business is profitable.
- **Key Sections**:
    - **Revenue**: Sales or income from products and services.
    - **Expenses**: Costs of goods sold, operational expenses, taxes, etc.

○ **Net Income**: The bottom line, representing profit or loss.

QuickBooks Process:

- **QuickBooks Online**: Go to **Reports** > **Profit and Loss**.
- **QuickBooks Desktop**: Go to **Reports** > **Company & Financial** > **Profit & Loss Standard**.

2. Balance Sheet

The Balance Sheet provides a snapshot of a business's financial position at a given point in time, summarizing assets, liabilities, and equity.

- **Purpose**: It helps assess the financial stability of a business by showing the relationship between assets, liabilities, and owners' equity.
- **Key Sections**:
    ○ **Assets**: What the business owns, such as cash, accounts receivable, inventory, and equipment.

- ○ **Liabilities**: What the business owes, such as loans and accounts payable.
- ○ **Equity**: The owner's share of the business, which is the difference between assets and liabilities.

QuickBooks Process:

- **QuickBooks Online**: Go to **Reports** > **Balance Sheet**.
- **QuickBooks Desktop**: Go to **Reports** > **Company & Financial** > **Balance Sheet Standard**.

3. Cash Flow Statement

The Cash Flow Statement tracks the flow of cash in and out of the business, categorized into operating, investing, and financing activities.

- **Purpose**: It helps business owners understand the liquidity position of the business, i.e., whether the business has enough cash to meet its obligations.
- **Key Sections**:

○ **Operating Activities**: Cash generated from day-to-day operations.

○ **Investing Activities**: Cash from buying or selling assets like equipment or investments.

○ **Financing Activities**: Cash flows from borrowing or repaying debt, issuing stock, or paying dividends.

QuickBooks Process:

- **QuickBooks Online**: Go to **Reports > Cash Flow**.

- **QuickBooks Desktop**: Go to **Reports > Company & Financial > Cash Flow Standard**.

4. Accounts Receivable Aging Report

The Accounts Receivable Aging report shows outstanding invoices and how long they have been overdue.

- **Purpose**: It helps businesses manage collections, track overdue invoices, and ensure customers are paying on time.
- **Key Sections**:
  - ○ **Aging Categories**: Typically includes 0-30 days, 31-60 days, and 60+ days.
  - ○ **Customer Details**: Names of customers, invoice amounts, and overdue periods.

QuickBooks Process:

- **QuickBooks Online**: Go to **Reports > Aged Receivables Summary**.
- **QuickBooks Desktop**: Go to **Reports > Customers & Receivables > A/R Aging Summary**.

5. Accounts Payable Aging Report

The Accounts Payable Aging report shows unpaid bills and how long they have been outstanding.

- **Purpose**: It helps businesses manage cash flow by ensuring bills are paid on time and identifying late payment risks.
- **Key Sections**:
  - **Aging Categories**: Includes 0-30 days, 31-60 days, and 60+ days.
  - **Vendor Details**: Names of vendors, bill amounts, and overdue periods.

QuickBooks Process:

- **QuickBooks Online**: Go to **Reports** > **Aged Payables Summary**.
- **QuickBooks Desktop**: Go to **Reports** > **Vendors & Payables** > **A/P Aging Summary**.

Customizing Reports for Business Needs

While QuickBooks provides powerful default reports, the ability to customize them is what sets the software apart. Customizing reports ensures that they are tailored to the specific needs of your business, making them more useful and actionable.

1. Customizing Report Filters

QuickBooks allows you to add and remove filters to reports based on specific needs, such as by date, customer, vendor, or account.

QuickBooks Online:

1. Run the report you want to customize.
2. Click the **Customize** button at the top.
3. Adjust filters like **Date Range**, **Account Type**, **Customer**, etc.
4. Click **Run Report** after applying the changes.

QuickBooks Desktop:

1. Open the report you want to customize.
2. Click **Customize Report**.
3. Use the **Display**, **Filters**, and **Header/Footer** tabs to modify the report.
4. Click **OK** to apply changes.

2. Adding or Removing Columns

For reports such as the Profit and Loss or Balance Sheet, QuickBooks allows you to add or remove columns to focus on the most important information.

- **Example**: If you only want to see expenses related to a specific department, you can remove all other categories and columns for clarity.

3. Custom Report Layouts

For businesses that want specific branding, QuickBooks provides the option to modify the layout of reports. You can add your business logo, change fonts, colors, and even adjust the layout of columns.

QuickBooks Online:

1. Customize a report and save it as a **Custom Report**.
2. Choose from available layout templates or adjust the layout settings manually.

QuickBooks Desktop:

1. Customize a report and save it under a new name.
2. Use the **Report Templates** option to select and modify layout designs.

Exporting and Sharing Reports

QuickBooks allows for easy export and sharing of reports, enabling business owners and accountants to analyze and share data with stakeholders.

1. Exporting Reports

QuickBooks provides various export options, including exporting reports to Excel, PDF, and CSV formats.

QuickBooks Online:

1. Open the report you want to export.

2. Click the **Export** button on the top-right corner of the report.
3. Choose **Export to Excel**, **Export to PDF**, or other available formats.

QuickBooks Desktop:

1. Open the desired report.
2. Click **Excel** > **Create New Worksheet** or **Export to PDF**.
3. Save the file in the desired location.

2. Sharing Reports with Stakeholders

QuickBooks allows you to email reports directly from the software.

QuickBooks Online:

1. Customize and run the report you want to share.
2. Click the **Email** button at the top of the report.
3. Enter the recipient's email address and add a message, then click **Send**.

QuickBooks Desktop:

1. Customize and run the report.
2. Click **Email** at the top.
3. Choose the email template, add the recipient's email address, and click **Send**.

3. Scheduling Reports for Regular Delivery

QuickBooks allows you to schedule reports to run and email them automatically at specific intervals, ensuring that you or stakeholders always have up-to-date data.

QuickBooks Online:

1. Go to **Reports**.
2. Open the desired report.
3. Click **Schedule** and set the frequency (daily, weekly, monthly).
4. Enter the recipients' emails and schedule the report.

QuickBooks Desktop:

1. Customize the report.

2. Go to **Reports** > **Scheduled Reports**.
3. Set the frequency and recipients, and then save the schedule.

Budgeting and Forecasting in QuickBooks

Effective budgeting and forecasting are essential for any business, enabling owners and managers to set financial goals, track progress, and make informed decisions for the future. QuickBooks offers powerful tools to streamline the process of budgeting, comparing actual performance to planned figures, and even forecasting future financial trends.

Creating Budgets in QuickBooks

A budget is a financial plan that outlines expected income, expenses, and cash flow for a specific period, such as a month, quarter, or year. QuickBooks allows users to easily create and manage budgets, giving businesses the tools to plan for various financial scenarios.

1. Setting Up a Budget in QuickBooks

Creating a budget in QuickBooks involves specifying your revenue, expenses, and profit goals for a designated period. You can create budgets for specific departments, categories, or even across the entire business.

QuickBooks Online:

1. **Navigate to Budgeting**: From the **Gear** icon in the top right, select **Budgeting** under the **Tools** section.
2. **Create a New Budget**: Click on the **Create New Budget** button.
3. **Choose a Budget Type**: You can select either **Profit and Loss** or **Balance Sheet**

as your budget type. Most businesses will opt for a Profit and Loss budget.

4. **Set the Date Range**: Choose the fiscal year or specific period for which you want to create the budget.

5. **Assign Accounts and Categories**: QuickBooks will automatically assign the appropriate accounts (e.g., income, expenses) based on your chart of accounts. You can adjust these as needed.

6. **Enter Budget Amounts**: Enter your target figures for each account (e.g., projected revenue, expenses, etc.) for each month or quarter.

7. **Save and Review**: Once you've filled in your budget details, click **Save** and review the budget to ensure accuracy.

QuickBooks Desktop:

1. Go to **Company** > **Planning & Budgeting** > **Set Up Budgets**.
2. Select the **Create New Budget** option.
3. Choose the **Fiscal Year** and decide whether you want to create a budget for

the entire company or for a specific class (e.g., by department or location).

4. Select the **Budget Period** (e.g., monthly, quarterly).

5. Enter your projected income and expense figures for each account or category.

6. Click **Finish** to save the budget.

2. Adjusting and Editing Budgets

Once your budget is created, you may find it necessary to adjust the figures as circumstances change. QuickBooks makes it easy to update your budget, whether you're adjusting for seasonal fluctuations or responding to new financial conditions.

QuickBooks Online:

1. Go to **Gear > Budgeting**.

2. Find and select the budget you want to adjust.

3. Click **Edit** and adjust your numbers as needed.

4. Save the updated budget.

QuickBooks Desktop:

1. Go to **Company** > **Planning & Budgeting** > **Set Up Budgets**.
2. Select the existing budget.
3. Make necessary changes and click **Finish** to save your adjustments.

Comparing Actuals Against Budgets

After setting up your budget, it's essential to monitor how actual financial performance compares to your planned budget. QuickBooks allows you to compare your actual income and expenses against budgeted amounts in real time, helping you stay on track and make adjustments when needed.

1. Running Budget vs. Actual Reports

QuickBooks provides a simple and effective way to generate reports comparing actual figures to your budgeted amounts. These reports help identify discrepancies and highlight areas that need attention.

QuickBooks Online:

1. Go to the **Reports** section.
2. In the search bar, type **Budget vs. Actual**.
3. Select the **Budget vs. Actuals** report.
4. Choose the budget and the date range you want to analyze.
5. Click **Run Report** to view a side-by-side comparison of actual income and expenses against the budgeted figures.

Key Features of the Report:

- **Actuals Column**: Shows your real income and expenses for the selected period.
- **Budgeted Column**: Displays the budgeted amounts for comparison.
- **Variance**: Highlights the difference between actuals and budgeted amounts, indicating whether you're over or under budget.

QuickBooks Desktop:

1. Go to **Reports** > **Company & Financial**.
2. Select **Budget vs. Actual**.
3. Choose the fiscal year, period, and the budget to compare.
4. View the report, which will show actual and budgeted amounts side by side.

2. Analyzing Variances

The variance is the difference between actual performance and the budgeted figures. QuickBooks helps you quickly spot variances in income and expenses, allowing you to analyze and adjust accordingly. Large variances in income or expenses could indicate that you need to revisit your budget or operational processes.

- **Positive Variance (Under Budget)**: When actual income exceeds budgeted income or actual expenses are lower than expected, it's considered a positive variance. This could indicate that you're outperforming your projections or controlling costs better than anticipated.

- **Negative Variance (Over Budget)**: A negative variance occurs when actual income is lower than expected or when actual expenses exceed the budgeted amounts. This could indicate potential financial issues, such as underperformance or overspending.

3. Adjusting Budgets Based on Actuals

If you notice recurring negative variances or if your financial outlook changes, you may need to adjust your budget. QuickBooks allows you to make real-time adjustments to your budget figures and can help you reallocate funds to meet changing business needs.

- **QuickBooks Online**: Navigate to **Budgeting** from the **Gear** icon and adjust your budget.
- **QuickBooks Desktop**: Go to **Company** > **Planning & Budgeting** > **Set Up Budgets** and edit the current budget.

Using Forecasting Tools in QuickBooks

Forecasting is the process of predicting future financial performance based on historical data, trends, and assumptions. QuickBooks offers tools to help you forecast revenue, expenses, and cash flow, enabling better financial planning and decision-making.

1. Using the Forecasting Feature in QuickBooks Online

QuickBooks Online's forecasting feature allows you to estimate your future financial performance based on past data. It provides projections for sales, expenses, and profit over a chosen period.

Steps to Use QuickBooks Online Forecasting:

1. Go to **Reports** and select **Forecast**.
2. QuickBooks will automatically generate a forecast based on your past data. You can

adjust the forecast period, accounts, and assumptions.

3. Review the forecasted figures for income and expenses.
4. Adjust assumptions such as growth rates, sales projections, and expense increases as needed.
5. Save and review the forecast periodically to track whether you're on target.

2. Customizing Forecasting for Specific Needs

While QuickBooks offers default forecasting tools based on historical data, businesses often need more tailored forecasting models. You can customize your forecasts by adjusting key assumptions or integrating external data for more accurate predictions.

- **Seasonal Adjustments**: If your business experiences seasonal fluctuations, adjust the forecast to reflect higher or lower sales in particular months.
- **Growth Rates**: Modify your forecast based on expected changes in sales,

business expansion, or other growth metrics.

3. Integrating Third-Party Forecasting Tools

For businesses that require more complex forecasting, QuickBooks can integrate with third-party forecasting tools and apps, such as Fathom, G-Accon, and Float. These integrations allow for more advanced financial models, including predictive analytics, which can enhance decision-making and provide more granular forecasts.

Inventory Management in QuickBooks

Effective inventory management is crucial for any business that deals with physical products. Whether you're managing a small business or a larger enterprise, having a streamlined system to track, adjust, and replenish inventory ensures that you maintain the right stock levels, reduce waste, and meet customer demand efficiently. QuickBooks offers robust inventory management tools that allow businesses to track stock, manage adjustments, and create purchase orders seamlessly. This section will cover the essential features for inventory management, including setting up and tracking inventory, managing inventory adjustments, and handling purchase orders.

Setting Up and Tracking Inventory in QuickBooks

1. Setting Up Inventory in QuickBooks

Before you can begin managing your inventory in QuickBooks, you need to set it up correctly. The setup process involves configuring your products, assigning inventory accounts, and ensuring that you have the right settings in place to track your items effectively.

QuickBooks Online:

1. **Enable Inventory Tracking:**

   o Go to the **Gear** icon and select **Account and Settings**.

- o Under the **Sales** tab, scroll down to the **Products and Services** section and toggle on **Track inventory quantity on hand**.
- o This allows QuickBooks to track inventory items and provide real-time updates on your stock levels.

2. **Add Inventory Items**:

- o Navigate to the **Sales** tab and click **Products and Services**.
- o Select **New** to add a new inventory item.
- o Choose **Inventory** as the type of product.
- o Enter a name for the product, SKU (if applicable), and description.
- o Specify the **purchase information**, including cost of goods sold (COGS) and preferred vendors.
- o Enter the **sales price** and **income account** for the item.

○ For the **inventory asset account**,
   choose the account where you want
   to track the value of your inventory.

3. **Track Inventory Quantity and Value**:

○ When you set up inventory items,
   QuickBooks allows you to enter the
   quantity on hand at the time of
   setup. QuickBooks will track the
   quantity and update the inventory as
   you make purchases or sales.
○ QuickBooks will also track the
   value of your inventory based on
   the **purchase cost** you've entered,
   updating the **inventory asset
   account** and **COGS** as transactions
   occur.

QuickBooks Desktop:

1. Go to **Edit** > **Preferences** > **Items &
   Inventory** > **Company Preferences**.

2. Check the box to enable **Inventory and purchase orders are active**.

3. Click **OK** to confirm and proceed with item setup.

4. **Create Inventory Items**:

   o Go to **Lists** > **Item List**.
   o Click **Item** > **New** and select **Inventory Part**.
   o Enter the item name, description, cost, and sales price.
   o Define the **inventory asset account** where QuickBooks will track the inventory value.
   o Specify the **COGS** account for expense tracking.

---

2. Tracking Inventory in QuickBooks

Once your inventory is set up, QuickBooks will automatically track quantities and costs as you make purchases or sales. Every time you buy or sell inventory items, QuickBooks will update the quantities and costs in real-time, ensuring that your inventory records are always accurate.

Tracking Inventory for Sales:

- When you create an invoice for a sale that includes inventory items, QuickBooks automatically reduces the stock quantity and records the corresponding sales transaction, including revenue and COGS.

Tracking Inventory for Purchases:

- When you receive an inventory item from a vendor, QuickBooks will update the quantity on hand and the inventory asset account. Any purchase invoices entered will also affect the cost of goods sold (COGS) and the inventory value.

QuickBooks Online:

- Go to **Sales** > **Products and Services** to view inventory items and their quantities.

- You can see the available quantity of each item, and QuickBooks will provide a warning if the quantity falls below the reorder point.

QuickBooks Desktop:

- Go to **Reports** > **Inventory** to view detailed inventory reports such as the **Inventory Valuation Summary**, **Inventory Stock Status by Item**, or **Inventory Turnover**.

Managing Inventory Adjustments

Inventory adjustments are a regular part of inventory management. These adjustments may be necessary due to damaged goods, lost inventory, changes in stock levels, or discrepancies between physical stock and recorded inventory. QuickBooks provides tools for making these adjustments, ensuring that your inventory levels and values remain accurate.

1. Making Inventory Adjustments in QuickBooks

Inventory adjustments in QuickBooks allow you to manually update inventory quantities or values, ensuring that your records align with actual stock levels.

QuickBooks Online:

1. Go to the **+ New** button and select **Inventory Qty Adjustment** under the **Other** section.
2. Select the **Adjustment Date** and the inventory account.
3. Choose the **Inventory Item** that needs adjustment.
4. Enter the **adjustment quantity** (positive for adding stock, negative for removing stock) and the **reason** for the adjustment (e.g., loss, damage, etc.).
5. Review the adjustment to ensure accuracy, then click **Save and Close**.

QuickBooks Desktop:

1. Go to **Vendors > Inventory Activities > Adjust Quantity/Value on Hand**.
2. Choose the **Adjustment Account** (usually the inventory asset account).
3. Select the **Item** to adjust, and enter the **quantity change** (positive or negative).
4. Provide the **reason** for the adjustment (optional) and save the adjustment.

2. Inventory Adjustment Reports

QuickBooks offers reports to track inventory adjustments, helping you identify patterns of inventory loss, damage, or theft.

QuickBooks Online:

- Go to **Reports > Inventory > Inventory Adjustment History** to see all adjustments made over time, including quantities adjusted, reasons, and amounts.

QuickBooks Desktop:

- Go to **Reports** > **Inventory** > **Inventory Adjustments** to generate an inventory adjustment report.

Handling Purchase Orders

Purchase orders (POs) are used to request inventory from suppliers and keep track of what items you need to buy. They serve as formal requests for goods or services, ensuring that you maintain proper stock levels. QuickBooks provides a streamlined process for creating and managing purchase orders.

1. Creating Purchase Orders in QuickBooks

A purchase order is created when you decide to order more inventory from a vendor. QuickBooks allows you to create POs, track their status, and convert them into bills once the order is received.

QuickBooks Online:

1. Go to the + **New** button and select **Purchase Order**.
2. Choose the **Vendor** from whom you're purchasing the items.
3. Add the **inventory items** you wish to order, along with quantities and prices.
4. Set the **delivery date** and include any additional terms.
5. Click **Save and Close** or **Save and Send** if you want to email the PO directly to the vendor.

QuickBooks Desktop:

1. Go to **Vendors > Create Purchase Orders**.
2. Select the **Vendor** and enter the inventory items, quantities, and pricing.
3. Specify the **ship-to address** and any other required details.
4. Click **Save & Close** when done.

2. Converting Purchase Orders to Bills

Once you receive the items from the vendor, you can convert the PO into a bill to process payment. This ensures that inventory levels are updated automatically, and the appropriate financial transactions are recorded.

QuickBooks Online:

1. Go to + **New** and select **Bill**.
2. Choose the **Vendor** and the **PO** you want to convert.
3. QuickBooks will automatically pull the items and quantities from the PO into the bill.
4. Review the details and click **Save and Close** or **Pay Bill**.

QuickBooks Desktop:

1. Go to **Vendors > Receive Items and Enter Bills**.
2. Select the **Vendor** and the **Purchase Order**.
3. QuickBooks will populate the items from the PO.

4. Click **Save & Close** once the bill is correct.

3. Tracking Purchase Orders and Receiving Inventory

QuickBooks allows you to track the status of each PO to ensure that you stay informed about what inventory has been ordered and received.

QuickBooks Online:

- You can view and manage your open purchase orders by navigating to **Expenses** > **Vendors** > **Purchase Orders**. This section shows the status of each PO (open, closed, etc.).

QuickBooks Desktop:

- Go to **Reports** > **Purchasing** > **Open Purchase Orders** to view all outstanding purchase orders.

QuickBooks Online vs. QuickBooks Desktop

When deciding between QuickBooks Online and QuickBooks Desktop, it's essential to understand how each version caters to different business needs. While both are designed to help small to mid-sized businesses manage their finances, they offer distinct advantages depending on factors such as the type of business, the need for mobility, and the level of customization required. This section explores the key differences between QuickBooks Online and QuickBooks Desktop, highlights the benefits of cloud-based solutions, and discusses the process of transitioning between platforms.

Key Differences Between Versions

1. Accessibility

- **QuickBooks Online**: QuickBooks Online (QBO) is a cloud-based accounting software that allows users to access their data from anywhere with an internet connection. Whether you're working in the office, at home, or on the go, you can access and manage your finances in real-time using any device (desktop, laptop, tablet, or smartphone).

  Key Feature: Real-time access and multi-device synchronization, making it ideal for businesses that need flexible, remote access.

- **QuickBooks Desktop**: QuickBooks Desktop is installed directly on a computer and can only be accessed from that device unless additional steps are taken, such as hosting the software on a server. Desktop versions generally require more infrastructure and are less accessible than their cloud counterparts. However, QuickBooks Desktop offers more powerful features in some cases.

Key Feature: Limited to the device it's installed on, unless additional setup (e.g., remote access or cloud hosting) is implemented.

2. Features and Customization

- **QuickBooks Online**: QuickBooks Online offers a wide range of features, including invoicing, expense tracking, tax calculations, and basic inventory management. It also integrates seamlessly with a variety of third-party apps, offering flexibility and scalability for businesses that need additional tools for managing their operations. The customization options are relatively limited compared to

QuickBooks Desktop, but QuickBooks Online continues to add more features and enhancements through updates.

Key Feature: Easy integration with third-party apps and automatic updates.

- **QuickBooks Desktop**: QuickBooks Desktop offers more advanced features, especially for businesses with complex accounting needs. These features include advanced inventory management, job costing, industry-specific versions (such as for manufacturing, retail, or construction), and customizable reports. Desktop allows for a higher degree of customization in terms of reporting, chart of accounts, and other accounting tasks, making it ideal for businesses with more intricate accounting requirements.

Key Feature: Advanced reporting, customization, and specialized industry features.

3. Pricing

- **QuickBooks Online**: QuickBooks Online follows a subscription-based pricing model, with several tiers based on the size of the business and the features needed. The subscription fee covers cloud hosting, customer support, and software updates. Pricing can be more predictable, and businesses can scale their subscription as needed.

   Key Feature: Monthly subscription-based pricing with flexible tiers and no upfront cost for software.

- **QuickBooks Desktop**: QuickBooks Desktop typically uses a one-time license fee for the software. However, if you want access to updates and support, you'll need to purchase an annual subscription, adding ongoing costs. The pricing for the

Desktop version is often higher upfront but can be more cost-effective in the long run if you don't need to upgrade or add additional features regularly.

Key Feature: One-time software purchase with optional annual fees for updates and support.

4. Updates and Support

- **QuickBooks Online**: One of the main advantages of QuickBooks Online is automatic updates. As a cloud-based solution, users always have access to the latest features, enhancements, and security updates without having to manually install anything. Support is available through chat, phone, and a large knowledge base.

  Key Feature: Automatic updates and cloud-based security management.

- **QuickBooks Desktop**: QuickBooks Desktop requires users to manually update the software, and these updates are typically released annually. While the updates often include new features and bug fixes, users must be proactive in ensuring they have the latest version. Additionally, support is provided through phone and live chat, but there is no automatic software updating mechanism.

  Key Feature: Manual updates and fewer automatic improvements compared to QuickBooks Online.

5. Integration and Add-ons

- **QuickBooks Online**: QuickBooks Online offers a robust marketplace of integrations with over 650 apps, allowing businesses to customize the software to fit their specific needs. These integrations include popular apps for payroll, CRM, point-of-sale, inventory, and more. The cloud-based nature of QBO ensures seamless connectivity with these third-party applications.

 Key Feature: Integration with hundreds of third-party apps, enhancing customization and scalability.

- **QuickBooks Desktop**: QuickBooks Desktop also offers a wide range of third-party integrations, but the setup can be more complicated than QuickBooks Online. Many add-ons require manual installation, and while many industry-specific tools are available, they may not be as easy to integrate or as seamlessly connected as those for QBO.

 Key Feature: Limited integration options compared to QuickBooks Online, but with deeper customization options.

Benefits of Cloud-Based Solutions

Cloud-based accounting solutions like QuickBooks Online offer several significant advantages over traditional desktop software. Here are some of the key benefits of using QuickBooks Online for your business:

1. Access Anytime, Anywhere

One of the most compelling reasons to use QuickBooks Online is its flexibility. As long as you have an internet connection, you can access your financial data from anywhere—be it your home, office, or while traveling. This is particularly beneficial for business owners who need to manage finances on the go or collaborate with team members remotely.

2. Automatic Backups and Security

Cloud-based systems automatically back up your data and protect it with advanced encryption. This means that your financial data is safer from theft, loss, or damage. QuickBooks Online's cloud infrastructure is equipped with industry-standard security measures to safeguard your business information, and you don't need to worry about manual backups or system crashes.

3. Collaboration Made Easy

Cloud software allows multiple users to access and work on the same set of data at the same time. QuickBooks Online supports team collaboration, so accountants, business owners, and other stakeholders can work simultaneously, without the need for syncing or sharing files back and forth.

4. Real-Time Updates and Features

With QuickBooks Online, updates are rolled out automatically, meaning your business always has the latest features and tools. This is a significant advantage for companies looking to stay ahead of the curve and leverage new technological advancements without needing to purchase new software or manually install updates.

5. Scalability and Flexibility

QuickBooks Online's subscription-based model allows businesses to scale their usage as needed. If you need more users or additional features, you can upgrade your subscription. Similarly, you can downgrade if your needs change, making QBO a flexible solution for businesses at different stages of growth.

Transitioning Between Platforms

While both QuickBooks Online and Desktop have their strengths, businesses may find themselves needing to transition between the two platforms for various reasons—such as growing business needs, changing technology preferences, or specific feature requirements. Transitioning from QuickBooks Desktop to QuickBooks Online, or vice versa, is possible but involves careful planning to ensure that no data is lost in the process.

1. Transitioning from QuickBooks Desktop to QuickBooks Online

QuickBooks offers a tool to convert data from QuickBooks Desktop to QuickBooks Online, simplifying the transition process. However, the following steps are essential:

- **Check Compatibility**: Some features in QuickBooks Desktop may not transfer directly to QuickBooks Online (e.g., complex inventory or job costing), so it's important to verify that the data you need will be supported in QBO.
- **Backup Your Data**: Before beginning the transition, ensure you create a backup of your QuickBooks Desktop data to prevent any data loss.
- **Use the QuickBooks Conversion Tool**: QuickBooks offers an easy-to-use conversion tool that can help you move your company file from Desktop to Online. Follow the steps outlined by QuickBooks to upload your file to QuickBooks Online.
- **Reconcile Accounts**: After migrating, carefully check your accounts, reports,

and transactions to ensure everything was transferred correctly.

2. Transitioning from QuickBooks Online to QuickBooks Desktop

Moving from QuickBooks Online to Desktop is more complicated and often requires manual intervention because QuickBooks doesn't offer a direct conversion tool for this process. You will need to export your data from QuickBooks Online and import it into QuickBooks Desktop. Here are the steps to take:

- **Export Reports**: Export financial reports, transactions, and customer/vendor details from QuickBooks Online to Excel or CSV files.
- **Manually Input Data into QuickBooks Desktop**: Import the necessary data into QuickBooks Desktop. You may need to recreate certain records, such as inventory levels or job costing data.
- **Set Up QuickBooks Desktop**: Once your data is transferred, set up your

QuickBooks Desktop company file and integrate any third-party apps that are compatible with the Desktop version.

QuickBooks Advanced Features

QuickBooks is a robust accounting software offering a variety of features that cater to different types of businesses. While the basic functionalities like invoicing, expense tracking, and reporting are essential, the advanced features of QuickBooks take accounting to the next level, enabling businesses to manage complex transactions, streamline project management, and extend the software's capabilities through third-party integrations.

Managing Multi-Currency Transactions

What Is Multi-Currency in QuickBooks?

Managing multi-currency transactions is crucial for businesses that deal with international clients, suppliers, or have multiple branches in different countries. QuickBooks offers a multi-currency feature, available in both QuickBooks Online and QuickBooks Desktop (Enterprise and certain other versions). This feature allows businesses to work with different currencies seamlessly while keeping accurate records of conversions, payments, and balances in their home currency.

Setting Up Multi-Currency in QuickBooks

To get started with multi-currency in QuickBooks, businesses must first enable the multi-currency option in their settings. The process varies slightly between the desktop and online versions:

- **In QuickBooks Online**: Go to **Settings > Account and Settings > Advanced**. Under the Currency section, click on

"Edit" and enable multi-currency. Once activated, QuickBooks will allow you to select different currencies when creating transactions.

- **In QuickBooks Desktop**: The process for enabling multi-currency is in the **Preferences** section. Navigate to **Edit > Preferences > Multiple Currencies**, and then select "Yes" to allow the use of multiple currencies.

Once multi-currency is enabled, businesses can select a currency for every customer, vendor, or account, and QuickBooks will automatically calculate currency conversions based on exchange rates.

Key Features of Multi-Currency in QuickBooks

1. **Automatic Currency Conversion**: When creating transactions with foreign customers or suppliers, QuickBooks will

automatically convert the amounts from the selected foreign currency to your home currency. This eliminates the need for manual conversions and reduces the risk of errors.

2. **Exchange Rate Tracking**: QuickBooks allows you to set up exchange rates and even adjust them manually if needed. The software updates exchange rates automatically, but businesses can change them based on the latest market fluctuations or negotiation rates with foreign clients or vendors.

3. **Multi-Currency Reporting**: Multi-currency transactions can be tracked and reported in the correct currency. QuickBooks generates accurate reports that display figures in both your home currency and the transaction currency, ensuring that financial statements, such as Profit & Loss or Balance Sheet, reflect the

correct data.

4. **Revaluation of Foreign Currency Balances**: QuickBooks allows you to adjust the value of foreign currency balances due to changes in the exchange rate. This ensures that your financial reports are accurate and reflect any adjustments in the value of foreign currency assets and liabilities.

5. **Invoicing and Payments in Foreign Currency**: QuickBooks enables users to create invoices and receive payments in foreign currencies, reducing the administrative burden and streamlining the payment process for international transactions.

Benefits of Multi-Currency in QuickBooks

- **Accurate Financial Records**: Multi-currency functionality ensures that businesses are always in compliance with

accounting standards by accurately
tracking foreign transactions.

- **Saves Time**: Automatic exchange rate
  tracking and currency conversion reduce
  manual work and errors in currency
  calculations.
- **Global Business Management**: The
  ability to handle multiple currencies helps
  businesses expand globally without
  having to use complex external systems.

Using QuickBooks for Project Tracking

What Is Project Tracking in QuickBooks?

Project tracking allows businesses to monitor the
progress, profitability, and expenses of specific
projects or jobs. This feature is particularly
useful for service-based industries, construction,
and project-based work, where tracking
expenses, billing, and progress for individual
projects is crucial for profitability.

Setting Up Projects in QuickBooks

QuickBooks makes it easy to track projects by allowing users to create a "project" within the software. This functionality is available in both QuickBooks Online (with Plus and Advanced versions) and QuickBooks Desktop (Premier, Enterprise, and certain other versions).

To set up project tracking:

- **In QuickBooks Online**: Navigate to **Projects** from the left-hand sidebar, then click "Create Project." You will be prompted to enter the project's name and details. From there, you can associate the project with specific customers and track transactions related to the project.

- **In QuickBooks Desktop**: QuickBooks Desktop allows for job costing. To track projects, go to **Customers > Create Jobs**, and link them to your customers. From there, you can associate transactions with specific jobs and track income and expenses for each job.

Key Features of Project Tracking in QuickBooks

1. **Job Costing**: QuickBooks allows businesses to assign and track all costs associated with a specific job or project. This includes labor, materials, and overhead. Job costing helps businesses determine the exact profitability of each project by comparing the total costs with the revenue earned.

2. **Invoicing for Projects**: Once a project is underway, QuickBooks enables businesses to create and send invoices related to the project. You can break down the project's billing based on tasks, materials, or milestones, helping to ensure that billing is aligned with the project's progress.

3. **Tracking Time and Expenses**: QuickBooks allows you to track both time

and expenses for individual projects. You can create timesheets for employees working on the project, record billable hours, and assign those hours to specific tasks. Additionally, you can enter expenses like materials, subcontractor fees, or other project-related costs directly under the project.

4. **Project Profitability Reports**: QuickBooks provides a suite of reports to track the profitability of each project, including the **Profitability by Job** report. This report summarizes the income and costs associated with a project, allowing you to see whether a project is profitable or if you need to make adjustments.

5. **Milestone Tracking**: Projects can be broken down into milestones, allowing businesses to track progress toward completion. QuickBooks makes it easier to manage each milestone by creating specific budgets, tracking costs, and

invoicing clients according to these stages.

Benefits of Project Tracking in QuickBooks

- **Increased Transparency**: Project tracking ensures that all team members, stakeholders, and clients are aligned on the progress and financials of each project.
- **Better Profitability Insight**: You can gain clear insight into whether a project is operating within budget, allowing for more accurate forecasting and more effective decision-making.
- **Efficient Billing**: QuickBooks streamlines the billing process by associating invoices with specific projects, ensuring timely and accurate invoicing based on the work completed.

Integrating Third-Party Apps

What Are Third-Party Integrations?

QuickBooks offers powerful core functionality, but many businesses also rely on additional tools and services to manage their operations. Integrating third-party apps with QuickBooks can help businesses extend their capabilities, streamline workflows, and improve efficiency.

QuickBooks integrates with hundreds of third-party apps, including tools for customer relationship management (CRM), payroll, inventory management, e-commerce, time tracking, and more. These integrations allow businesses to work seamlessly across multiple platforms while keeping their financial data centralized within QuickBooks.

Setting Up Third-Party Integrations

To integrate third-party apps with QuickBooks, businesses can use the **QuickBooks App Store**, where a wide selection of apps is available. Integrations can be easily set up by connecting QuickBooks to the app through the App Store interface, and many integrations are designed to sync data automatically, reducing manual entry and errors.

Steps to integrate an app:

- Go to the **QuickBooks App Store**.
- Browse or search for the app you want to integrate with QuickBooks.
- Follow the prompts to connect your QuickBooks account with the third-party app.
- Review the data permissions and sync settings to ensure proper integration.

Key Benefits of Third-Party Integrations

1. **Enhanced Functionality**: By integrating QuickBooks with specialized apps, businesses can add functionality like CRM for better customer management, inventory tracking for real-time stock updates, and e-commerce for seamless integration with online stores.

2. **Data Syncing**: Automatic data syncing between QuickBooks and third-party apps ensures that your financial information is always up to date, eliminating the need for double data entry and minimizing human errors.

3. **Improved Efficiency**: Integrating QuickBooks with other business tools helps to automate workflows and reduce the time spent on manual data entry. This can significantly improve efficiency across various departments.

4. **Better Decision-Making**: Access to integrated data allows business owners to make better-informed decisions. For example, integration with a sales platform can provide real-time sales data, helping managers forecast revenue and adjust expenses accordingly.

Popular Third-Party Integrations with QuickBooks

- **Payroll**: QuickBooks integrates with payroll providers like Gusto and ADP, enabling seamless payroll management without the need for separate systems.
- **E-commerce**: Integrations with platforms like Shopify, Etsy, and Amazon help businesses sync sales and payment data between their online stores and QuickBooks.
- **Time Tracking**: Apps like TSheets allow businesses to track employee hours and automatically integrate that data into QuickBooks for easy payroll and billing.
- **CRM**: Integrations with tools like Salesforce or HubSpot help manage customer relationships and automate sales processes directly from QuickBooks.

Troubleshooting Common Issues in QuickBooks

Even though QuickBooks is designed to be user-friendly and efficient, users may occasionally encounter errors or face difficulties while navigating the software. Troubleshooting is an essential part of maintaining a smooth workflow and ensuring that QuickBooks continues to operate optimally. In this section, we will discuss common issues users face in QuickBooks, how to resolve them, how to back up and restore data, and how to access

QuickBooks support for more complex problems.

Resolving Common Errors

1. Company File Not Opening

One of the most frequent issues QuickBooks users face is being unable to open their company file. This can happen due to a variety of reasons, including corruption of the file or network-related issues. Here are some steps to troubleshoot:

Possible Solutions:

- **Check for Damaged Files**: If the file doesn't open, QuickBooks might display a message indicating file damage. You can use the **QuickBooks File Doctor** tool, a free utility provided by Intuit to diagnose and fix errors with QuickBooks files.

- **Repair QuickBooks**: Sometimes QuickBooks itself may need a repair. Go to **Control Panel > Programs > Programs and Features**, find QuickBooks, and select **Repair**. This process may take several minutes, and it will attempt to fix any installation issues.

- **Restore a Backup**: If the company file is damaged beyond repair, you may need to restore a backup. Be sure to regularly create backups of your QuickBooks company file to prevent loss of important data.

- **Update QuickBooks**: Make sure your QuickBooks is up to date. Intuit frequently releases updates that resolve bugs and fix compatibility issues with the operating system. Go to **Help > Update QuickBooks Desktop** to check for the latest updates.

2. Errors with Data Import or Export

Sometimes, QuickBooks users encounter errors when importing or exporting data between QuickBooks and third-party software. This can occur when the file format is incorrect, the data is corrupted, or there's a mismatch in versions.

Possible Solutions:

- **Check File Format**: Ensure that the data you are importing or exporting is in the correct file format. For example, QuickBooks supports importing data in **.IIF, .CSV**, or **.QBO** formats depending on the type of data.

- **Use the Import Utility**: QuickBooks provides an import utility for a variety of data types. Ensure you are using the right tool to import lists or transactions, and always match the fields in your import file to those in QuickBooks.

- **Verify Compatibility**: If exporting data, check that the third-party software you're using is compatible with QuickBooks. Some third-party applications require specific versions of QuickBooks to integrate properly.

---

3. Login Issues

It is common for users to forget passwords or face login issues when trying to access their QuickBooks account, especially when using QuickBooks Online or QuickBooks Desktop with a cloud-based version.

Possible Solutions:

- **Reset Password**: For QuickBooks Online, you can reset your password by clicking on the "Forgot Password" link on the login page. Follow the steps in the email sent to you to reset your password.

- **Check User Permissions**: If you are a company administrator, ensure that you have the correct permissions set up for users trying to log in. Sometimes, users may not have the right permissions to access certain features.

- **Clear Cache and Cookies**: Sometimes, login issues can occur due to corrupted browser cache and cookies. Clear your browser's cache and cookies or try logging in from a different browser.

---

4. QuickBooks Freezing or Running Slowly

If QuickBooks is freezing or running slowly, it can be caused by several factors, including system performance issues, insufficient RAM, or multiple users accessing the same file simultaneously.

Possible Solutions:

- **Check System Requirements**: Ensure your system meets the minimum and recommended system requirements for QuickBooks. If your computer is running low on resources (RAM or hard drive space), QuickBooks may not function properly.

- **Close Unnecessary Programs**: Closing unnecessary applications running in the background can free up system resources and improve QuickBooks performance.

- **Upgrade Your Hardware**: If QuickBooks continues to slow down, it may be time to upgrade your computer's hardware, such as adding more RAM or switching to a faster hard drive (SSD).

- **Optimize QuickBooks File**: QuickBooks offers a **File Optimization** tool, which can help speed up the software by reducing file size and clearing unnecessary data.

Backing Up and Restoring Data

Backing up your QuickBooks data is essential for protecting your financial records from unexpected loss. Regular backups ensure that you can restore your data if your system crashes, the company file is damaged, or if there are accidental data deletions.

Backing Up QuickBooks Data

Manual Backup

- **QuickBooks Online**: QuickBooks Online automatically backs up your data every 24 hours. However, it's still a good practice to periodically export your data. You can do this by going to **Settings > Back Up Data** and following the on-screen instructions.

- **QuickBooks Desktop**: To back up a company file in QuickBooks Desktop, go to **File > Back Up Company > Create Local Backup**. You can select between creating a backup on your computer or to an external drive or cloud storage (like Dropbox or Google Drive).

Automated Backups:

- **QuickBooks Online** automatically backs up your data daily, so you don't need to worry about manual backups.
- **QuickBooks Desktop** users can set up an automated backup schedule by going to **File > Back Up Company > Set Up Auto Backup**. This ensures your data is backed up regularly.

Restoring Data

If you need to restore a backup in QuickBooks, the process will vary depending on the version you're using:

Restoring from Backup in QuickBooks Online:

For QuickBooks Online, you can restore a version of your data from the **Audit Log**, which shows all changes made to your data. You can select an earlier version of the company data and restore it. Note that data restoration in QuickBooks Online is limited to a specific period.

Restoring from Backup in QuickBooks Desktop:

In QuickBooks Desktop, to restore a company file:

1. Open QuickBooks and go to **File > Open or Restore Company**.
2. Choose **Restore a Backup Copy** and click **Next**.

3. Select **Local Backup** and locate your backup file (.QBB).
4. Follow the prompts to restore the file.

Make sure that you are restoring the correct version of the backup to avoid overwriting important data.

Accessing QuickBooks Support

When troubleshooting issues in QuickBooks, if the above solutions don't resolve your problem, QuickBooks offers several support options to help you get back on track.

1. QuickBooks Help Menu

QuickBooks provides built-in help options, which are the first line of support for most issues. You can access the help menu by clicking on the **Help** icon in the top right corner (for QuickBooks Online) or selecting **Help** from the menu bar (for QuickBooks Desktop). The help options include:

- **Search for Articles**: Enter a keyword related to the issue you are facing, and QuickBooks will return relevant articles and tutorials.
- **Chat with Support**: In QuickBooks Online, you can live chat with a support agent directly through the help menu.
- **Community Forums**: QuickBooks has an active online community where users post questions and answers. You may find that someone else has already encountered the same issue and found a solution.

2. Contacting QuickBooks Support

If the issue is more complex and cannot be resolved through the Help menu, you can contact QuickBooks Support directly. Support options include:

- **Phone Support**: QuickBooks provides phone support for both QuickBooks Online and Desktop users. You can find the appropriate number for your region by visiting the **QuickBooks Support page**.

- **Live Chat**: QuickBooks Online users can chat with a support agent in real time through the help menu in the software.

- **Email**: For some versions of QuickBooks, you may be able to email support directly for help with your issue. QuickBooks will typically respond within 24 hours.

3. QuickBooks ProAdvisor

For businesses needing more specialized help, QuickBooks offers a network of **QuickBooks ProAdvisors**. These are certified accounting professionals who specialize in QuickBooks and can provide personalized support. ProAdvisors can help with:

- Installation and setup.
- Troubleshooting advanced issues.
- Accounting and bookkeeping advice.

- Ongoing QuickBooks training and support.

To find a QuickBooks ProAdvisor, visit the **Find a ProAdvisor** page on the QuickBooks website.

QuickBooks for Different Industries

QuickBooks is a versatile accounting software that can be customized to meet the specific needs of businesses in a wide range of industries. Whether you run a retail operation, a service-based company, or a nonprofit organization, QuickBooks offers powerful features and tools to streamline financial management.

Customizing QuickBooks for Retail Businesses

Retail businesses often face unique challenges when it comes to managing inventory, processing sales, and handling customer transactions. QuickBooks provides specialized tools and features designed to streamline operations for retailers, ensuring they can effectively manage their finances while focusing on customer satisfaction and growth.

Key Customization Options for Retailers:

1. **Inventory Management**:

   ○ **Track Inventory in Real-Time**: QuickBooks allows retailers to track inventory levels in real-time, which is crucial for maintaining stock levels and preventing overstocking or stockouts. By setting up inventory items in QuickBooks, retailers can easily monitor quantities, cost of goods sold (COGS), and manage pricing.
   ○ **Setting Up Inventory Items**: Retailers can create inventory

items, assign them to specific accounts (like income or expense accounts), and link them to sales transactions. QuickBooks also supports inventory tracking by using barcode scanning, which improves accuracy during sales transactions.

2. **Point of Sale (POS) Integration**:

   o **Integration with QuickBooks POS**: Retailers can integrate QuickBooks with a point-of-sale (POS) system, such as QuickBooks POS, to automatically sync sales data, inventory updates, and customer information. This integration reduces manual data entry and ensures real-time financial reporting.
   o **Sales and Returns**: QuickBooks tracks sales and returns, including discounts, taxes, and special pricing. Retailers can easily

generate sales reports and analyze trends in customer purchasing behavior.

3. **Managing Sales Taxes**:

   ○ **Sales Tax Tracking**: Retail businesses are required to collect and remit sales tax based on their location. QuickBooks allows retailers to set up sales tax rates by state, county, or city, and automatically apply them during transactions. Retailers can also generate sales tax reports to ensure compliance with local tax laws.
   ○ **Sales Tax Exemption**: For businesses selling to tax-exempt organizations, QuickBooks allows the option to set up exemptions, ensuring that no sales tax is charged on eligible transactions.

4. **Customizing Invoices and Receipts**:

- **Custom Templates**: Retailers can customize invoice and receipt templates to match their branding. QuickBooks provides options to add logos, change fonts, and include specific payment terms or conditions, making invoices and receipts professional and aligned with the store's image.

5. **Reports for Retailers**:

- **Sales Reports**: QuickBooks generates detailed sales reports, which help retailers track revenue and identify best-selling products. By analyzing sales data, businesses can optimize inventory, pricing, and promotional strategies.
- **Inventory Valuation and Profitability**: Retailers can view reports that track the value of their inventory, cost of goods sold, and profit margins. These reports provide insights into product

performance, ensuring that inventory management is efficient and cost-effective.

By leveraging QuickBooks' inventory and sales features, retailers can enhance operational efficiency, improve inventory control, and gain valuable insights into their business performance.

Adapting QuickBooks for Service-Based Companies

Service-based businesses, such as consulting firms, marketing agencies, law offices, and repair services, have different accounting needs compared to product-based businesses. These companies typically deal with billable hours, projects, contracts, and variable service fees, which require precise tracking and invoicing. QuickBooks can be customized to address these specific requirements, making it easier for service-based businesses to manage their financials.

Key Customization Options for Service-Based Companies:

1. **Tracking Billable Hours**:

   - **Time Tracking**: QuickBooks allows service-based businesses to track billable hours for employees or contractors. Users can log hours directly in QuickBooks and associate them with specific clients, jobs, or projects. This makes it easy to generate accurate invoices based on hourly rates.

   - **Integration with Time-Tracking Software**: QuickBooks integrates with popular time-tracking apps such as TSheets or QuickBooks Time, which allow employees to log time from anywhere and sync the data with QuickBooks automatically. This reduces errors and ensures that all billable hours are captured.

2. **Project and Job Costing**:

   ○ **Track Jobs and Projects**: QuickBooks enables service-based businesses to create projects and track the costs associated with each project or job. You can allocate expenses such as labor, materials, and overheads to specific jobs, making it easier to assess the profitability of each project.

   ○ **Job Profitability Reports**: QuickBooks generates reports that show the profitability of each project. These reports can help service businesses make informed decisions, allocate resources efficiently, and identify areas where costs can be reduced.

3. **Customizing Invoices for Service-Based Businesses**:

○ **Service Invoices**: Service-based companies can create custom invoices in QuickBooks that itemize the specific services provided. QuickBooks allows users to include descriptions, hourly rates, fixed fees, or any additional charges, and clients can be invoiced based on a specific project or service type.

○ **Recurring Billing**: For businesses that offer ongoing services (such as subscriptions or retainers), QuickBooks supports recurring billing. You can set up automated invoicing to charge clients at regular intervals, reducing administrative overhead.

4. **Managing Expenses and Payments**:

○ **Tracking Expenses**: QuickBooks allows service-based companies to track expenses associated with each job or project. Whether it's for materials, subcontractors, or travel, all costs can be allocated to specific projects for accurate cost tracking and profitability analysis.

- ○ **Billable Expenses**: Service companies can also charge clients for certain expenses incurred during the course of a project. QuickBooks allows users to mark specific expenses as billable, ensuring clients are reimbursed for costs such as travel, materials, or third-party services.

5. **Reports for Service-Based Businesses**:

- ○ **Profit and Loss by Job**: QuickBooks enables service businesses to generate Profit and Loss reports for each job or project. This helps to track income and expenses and measure the profitability of specific jobs or clients.

○ **Time and Expense Reports**:
Service-based companies can
generate time-tracking and expense
reports to ensure accurate billing.
This can include reports on billable
hours, billable expenses, and
client-specific projects.

By customizing QuickBooks for service-based
businesses, companies can effectively manage
their projects, track billable hours and expenses,
and streamline invoicing and payments.

Using QuickBooks in Nonprofits

Nonprofit organizations have specific financial
management needs due to their reliance on
donations, grants, and the need to adhere to strict
reporting standards. QuickBooks can be tailored
to meet the needs of nonprofits by providing
tools for tracking funds, managing grants, and
generating detailed reports for donors, board
members, and government agencies.

Key Customization Options for Nonprofits:

1. Tracking Donations and Grants:

- **Record Donations**: QuickBooks allows nonprofits to track donations from individuals, foundations, and corporations. Donations can be categorized by type (e.g., cash, in-kind) and associated with specific programs or projects.
- **Tracking Pledges and Grants**: Nonprofits can track pledges, grants, and restricted funds to ensure proper reporting and compliance. QuickBooks allows you to allocate donations to specific funds or programs and restrict their use as per donor specifications.

2. Class Tracking:

- **Program and Fund Tracking**: Nonprofits often run multiple programs and need to track the income and expenses for each one separately. QuickBooks offers a feature called **Classes** that allows users to categorize financial transactions by program or fund. This provides better visibility into how resources are being used across different areas of the organization.

○ **Donor and Campaign Tracking**: Nonprofits can track contributions by donor or campaign, providing insight into which fundraising efforts are the most successful and where additional focus is needed.

3. **Generating Donor and Tax Reports**:

○ **Donor Reports**: QuickBooks helps nonprofits generate detailed donor reports for acknowledgment letters, tax receipts, or end-of-year statements. The software allows organizations to easily create and customize donation receipts for tax purposes.

- ○ **Tax-Exempt Status Reporting**:
  Nonprofits need to provide reports
  on their tax-exempt status, ensuring
  that income from donations, grants,
  and fundraising events is properly
  categorized. QuickBooks provides
  specialized reports such as
  Statement of Activities and
  Statement of Financial Position to
  track funds and ensure compliance
  with IRS regulations.

4. **Budgeting and Fundraising Reports**:

  - ○ **Create Budgets for Programs**:
    QuickBooks allows nonprofits to
    create budgets for different
    programs and departments. By
    setting up budget categories,
    organizations can compare actual
    spending to budgeted figures,
    helping them stay within their
    financial goals.
  - ○ **Fundraising Reports**: Nonprofits
    can track fundraising events and

campaigns in QuickBooks, ensuring accurate records of donations, ticket sales, and expenses. This helps with transparency and accountability for donors.

5. **Tracking Volunteer Hours**:

   o **Volunteer Tracking**: While QuickBooks does not natively offer a volunteer tracking feature, many nonprofits use third-party integrations or manual entries to track volunteer hours. This allows nonprofits to report on in-kind contributions and offer recognition to volunteers.

Security and Data Protection in QuickBooks

Security and data protection are critical concerns for businesses that use QuickBooks, as the software handles sensitive financial information, including transactions, tax details, and customer data. Proper security measures are essential to prevent unauthorized access, data loss, and potential financial fraud. In this section, we will cover the importance of securing your QuickBooks data, how to set up user roles and permissions, and best practices for protecting your financial information through backups and data recovery.

Setting Up User Roles and Permissions

QuickBooks allows businesses to manage multiple users who have different roles and responsibilities within the company. Whether you are a small business owner, a manager, or an accountant, controlling who has access to specific data and functions is essential for maintaining security and preventing unauthorized actions.

1. User Roles and Permissions Overview

In QuickBooks, a **user role** refers to the specific set of permissions that determine what a user can see and do within the software. Permissions are categorized based on the tasks a user needs to perform, such as creating invoices, viewing reports, or managing payroll.

QuickBooks provides a wide range of roles, from general access for the business owner or accountant to limited access for employees who only need to view certain reports or enter sales transactions. By assigning appropriate roles and permissions, you can ensure that each user has access only to the features they need, and sensitive financial data remains protected.

2. Creating Users in QuickBooks

To set up users in QuickBooks, follow these steps:

- **QuickBooks Desktop**: Go to the "Company" menu, select "Set Up Users and Passwords," and choose "Set Up Users." From here, you can create new users and assign them to specific roles.
- **QuickBooks Online**: Navigate to the "Gear" icon and select "Manage Users" under the "Your Company" section. Click on "Add User" and follow the prompts to assign user roles and permissions.

You can customize roles for different team members by selecting predefined roles (such as "Admin," "Sales," "Accountant," or "Employee") or creating custom roles that fit your specific needs. **Admin roles** typically have full access to all features, while other roles may have limited access to particular areas, such as sales data, payroll, or reporting.

3. Permissions by Role

Each user role in QuickBooks comes with a pre-defined set of permissions, but you can adjust these permissions to grant more or less access. Key permissions include:

- **View Only**: Allow the user to view data without making any changes.
- **Create and Edit**: Permit the user to create and modify records, such as invoices or customer profiles.
- **Delete**: Grant permission to delete records, which should be restricted to administrators or high-level users.

- **Reports Access**: Specify whether a user can view or generate financial reports like balance sheets, profit & loss statements, and payroll reports.

By carefully managing roles and permissions, you can restrict access to sensitive data, minimize the risk of accidental or malicious actions, and ensure compliance with regulatory standards.

Protecting Your Financial Data

Your business's financial data is one of its most valuable assets, and safeguarding this information is paramount. QuickBooks offers various features and tools to protect your financial records from unauthorized access, data breaches, and potential cyber threats.

1. Password Protection and Authentication

One of the first lines of defense in securing QuickBooks data is **password protection**.

Ensure that every user has a strong, unique password, and require frequent password changes to mitigate the risk of unauthorized access.

For **QuickBooks Online**, consider enabling **two-factor authentication (2FA)**, which adds an extra layer of protection by requiring a second form of identification (such as a code sent to your phone) in addition to the regular password.

For **QuickBooks Desktop**, users should set up a secure password when creating the company file and ensure that the password meets strong criteria (including upper and lower case letters, numbers, and special characters). Make sure all employees use their own unique passwords, rather than sharing credentials, to further protect data.

2. Limit Access to Sensitive Information

As mentioned earlier, it's important to use QuickBooks' **role-based permissions** to limit user access to sensitive financial information. For example, an employee in sales might not need access to detailed financial reports, while an accountant or business owner should have full access to all data.

Be mindful of which users have access to:

- **Banking and payment information**: Limit access to bank account details, payment methods, and transfers.
- **Payroll data**: Restrict access to payroll information to ensure that only authorized personnel can view or modify payroll records.
- **Tax information**: Limit who can view and file tax-related data to protect your business from fraud or data manipulation.

3. Secure Your Devices and Networks

Securing the devices and networks that access QuickBooks is just as important as securing the software itself. Ensure that all devices—such as computers, smartphones, and tablets—are equipped with up-to-date antivirus software, firewalls, and encryption tools to protect against malware and unauthorized access.

In addition, consider using a **virtual private network (VPN)** for remote employees to encrypt internet traffic and protect sensitive data from cyber threats.

4. Regular Software Updates and Patches

QuickBooks releases regular updates and security patches to address any vulnerabilities in the software. Always make sure that you are using the latest version of QuickBooks, whether it's **QuickBooks Online** or **QuickBooks Desktop**, to take advantage of enhanced security features.

QuickBooks will notify users when updates are available, but it's also a good practice to check for updates manually by visiting the official QuickBooks website or using the built-in update feature in the software.

Regular Backups and Data Recovery

Despite your best efforts to protect your data, accidents and technical failures can still occur. Whether it's due to hardware failure, software issues, or cyberattacks, having a reliable backup and recovery strategy in place ensures that you can restore your data and minimize disruption.

1. Creating Regular Backups

Regular backups are vital for ensuring that you have access to a copy of your financial data in the event of an emergency. QuickBooks offers several backup options, depending on the version you are using.

- **QuickBooks Desktop**: In QuickBooks Desktop, you can manually back up your company file by going to the "File" menu and selecting "Back Up." You can also set up automatic backups to ensure that your data is regularly backed up without requiring manual intervention.

- **QuickBooks Online**: QuickBooks Online automatically saves your data in the cloud, but it's still a good idea to periodically export and save critical reports, such as balance sheets and profit & loss statements, to a secure external storage solution.

You can choose to back up your QuickBooks data to a local storage device, such as an external hard drive, or use cloud storage services for added protection. Cloud-based backups provide extra security in case of physical damage or theft, as the data is stored remotely.

2. Automating Backups

To minimize the risk of forgetting to back up your data, you can automate backups in QuickBooks. QuickBooks Online automatically backs up your data to the cloud, but for QuickBooks Desktop, you can schedule automatic backups using third-party cloud backup services, or by using QuickBooks' built-in scheduler to back up your data at regular intervals.

3. Data Recovery and Restoration

In the event that you need to restore your data, QuickBooks makes it relatively easy to recover from a backup.

- **QuickBooks Desktop**: If your QuickBooks Desktop file becomes damaged or lost, you can restore it by navigating to the "File" menu and selecting "Open or Restore Company." Then, choose the "Restore a Backup" option and select the backup file you wish to restore. Always keep a few recent backup copies to ensure you have access to the most up-to-date version of your financial data.

- **QuickBooks Online**: QuickBooks Online automatically syncs your data to the cloud, so your information is typically safe in the event of a device failure.

However, if you need to restore specific information, QuickBooks Online supports limited **transaction history recovery**. For comprehensive recovery, you may need to contact QuickBooks support for assistance.

4. Testing Your Backups

It's not enough to simply back up your data; you should regularly test your backups to ensure they are working properly. Try restoring a backup file to verify that the process works smoothly and that the data is intact.

QuickBooks Tips and Tricks

Mastering QuickBooks can be a game-changer for business owners and accountants, helping streamline accounting processes, save time, and reduce errors. Whether you're new to QuickBooks or an experienced user, there are plenty of tips and tricks that can help you become more efficient and accurate. In this section, we'll explore time-saving shortcuts, automation tools to handle repetitive tasks, and best practices to ensure your financial records are precise.

Time-Saving Shortcuts

QuickBooks is a robust software with numerous features that can sometimes be overwhelming. Luckily, several shortcuts and tips can help you navigate the software more efficiently, speeding up your workflow and reducing the time spent on mundane tasks.

1. Keyboard Shortcuts for Quick Navigation

- **Ctrl + 1**: Open the Company Information window.
- **Ctrl + 2**: Open the QuickBooks home page.
- **Ctrl + I**: Create a new invoice.
- **Ctrl + W**: Open the Write Checks window.
- **Ctrl + E**: Edit the selected transaction.
- **Ctrl + T**: Open the Transaction History for the selected customer or vendor.
- **Ctrl + F**: Open the Find window, allowing you to search for transactions by keyword or account.

These shortcuts significantly speed up daily operations and reduce the need to search through menus. As you get familiar with them, you'll notice a marked improvement in the time it takes to perform tasks.

2. Customizing Keyboard Shortcuts (QuickBooks Desktop)

If you frequently use certain functions, QuickBooks Desktop allows you to customize keyboard shortcuts. For example:

- Navigate to **Edit > Preferences > General**.
- Under the **My Preferences** tab, you can assign specific tasks or reports to customized keyboard shortcuts, making it even easier to access them.

3. Memorize Reports and Transactions

QuickBooks allows you to memorize reports and transactions that you use regularly. By memorizing reports, you can access them with just a few clicks without needing to configure filters or settings every time.

- **To Memorize a Report**: Run a report, then click **Memorize** at the top of the report window.
- **To Memorize a Transaction**: When creating a recurring invoice or bill, select **Make Recurring** in the transaction window to save it as a template.

This function is incredibly useful for businesses that need to generate the same reports or send the same invoices regularly.

Automating Repetitive Tasks

Automation can save you a lot of time and reduce errors, particularly for tasks that need to be done regularly. QuickBooks offers several features to automate processes, helping you focus on other aspects of your business.

1. Recurring Transactions

QuickBooks allows you to set up recurring transactions for tasks like invoices, bills, and journal entries. Instead of manually entering the same data every month, you can automate the process.

- **To Set Up Recurring Transactions**:
  1. Go to **Lists > Recurring Transactions**.
  2. Click **New** and select the type of transaction (Invoice, Bill, etc.).
  3. Choose a frequency (e.g., daily, weekly, monthly).
  4. Enter the details for the transaction, such as amounts and due dates.
  5. Click **OK** to save and QuickBooks will automatically generate these transactions according to the schedule.

By automating recurring invoices or bills, you can reduce manual data entry and ensure consistency in your accounting.

2. Automatic Bank Feeds (QuickBooks Online)

QuickBooks Online offers **bank feed integration**, where your bank transactions are automatically imported into QuickBooks. This eliminates the need for manual entry of every transaction.

- **To Set Up Bank Feeds**:
    1. Click the **Banking** tab and select **Bank Feeds**.
    2. Link your bank account by following the prompts.
    3. Once linked, QuickBooks will automatically import your bank transactions into the software.

Bank feeds can be used to match transactions with your QuickBooks records, categorize them, and reconcile accounts quickly, saving significant time.

3. Scheduled Reports (QuickBooks Online)

If you frequently need to review financial reports, QuickBooks Online allows you to schedule automatic reports. This feature is helpful for generating and receiving reports without having to manually create them each time.

- **To Schedule Reports**:
    1. Go to **Reports** and select the report you wish to schedule.
    2. Click **Save Customization** and choose **Set Schedule**.
    3. Choose the frequency and recipients for the report.

This feature ensures you have the financial information you need without constantly having to pull reports manually.

4. Payroll Automation (QuickBooks Online Payroll)

For businesses that run payroll frequently, QuickBooks Online Payroll offers automation for employee payments and tax filings. You can automate:

- **Employee Paychecks**: Set payroll to run automatically on specific dates.
- **Tax Calculations**: QuickBooks will automatically calculate and file payroll taxes for you.
- **Direct Deposit**: Employees can be paid via direct deposit automatically.

Automation in payroll helps avoid errors, ensures timely payments, and frees up administrative time.

Best Practices for Financial Accuracy

Accurate financial data is essential for making informed business decisions, meeting tax requirements, and ensuring the long-term success of your business. QuickBooks offers several tools and best practices to help maintain financial accuracy.

1. Regular Reconciliation

One of the most important steps in maintaining financial accuracy is regularly reconciling your accounts. Reconciliation ensures that the data in QuickBooks matches your bank and credit card statements.

- **Reconcile Bank Accounts**: Every month, review your bank feed and reconcile the transactions in QuickBooks. This prevents errors such as duplicate transactions or missed payments.
- **Reconcile Credit Cards**: Similarly, reconcile credit card accounts to ensure all charges and payments are accurately recorded.

By reconciling on a regular basis, you'll avoid discrepancies and ensure that your financial records are up to date.

2. Double-Check Data Entry

Errors often occur due to improper data entry. To prevent mistakes, it's important to double-check all manual entries, especially when entering bills, invoices, or journal entries. Look for common errors such as:

- Incorrect account selections
- Mistyped numbers
- Incorrect dates

Consider using **bank feeds** and **credit card feeds** to automatically import and categorize transactions, reducing manual entry errors.

3. Use Classes and Categories for Accuracy

QuickBooks allows you to use **classes** and **categories** to track and segment your financial data. By assigning specific classes to transactions, you can more accurately monitor different areas of your business, such as departments, locations, or product lines.

- **Set Up Classes**: In QuickBooks, go to **Edit > Preferences > Accounting** and enable **Class Tracking**. This will allow you to assign a class to each transaction to track specific business segments.

Proper categorization ensures that your financial reports reflect accurate and segmented data, giving you a clearer picture of your business's performance.

4. Maintain Consistent Naming Conventions

When creating customer profiles, vendor accounts, and products, it's essential to use consistent naming conventions. This practice makes it easier to find and organize records.

- **Use Descriptive Names**: Instead of generic names like "Customer 1" or "Vendor A," use clear, descriptive names to avoid confusion.
- **Standardize Product Codes**: If your business sells products, create a standardized system for product names and SKU codes.

Consistent naming helps avoid duplicate records and improves the searchability of your data.

5. Backup Your Data Regularly

A crucial part of maintaining financial accuracy is ensuring that you don't lose any valuable data. Make sure to **back up** your QuickBooks company files regularly.

- **QuickBooks Desktop**: Set up automatic backups to an external drive or cloud storage.
- **QuickBooks Online**: QuickBooks Online automatically saves your data in the cloud, but consider exporting key reports or downloading backups periodically to have an additional copy.

Backups ensure that your financial data is protected in case of a system crash or data corruption.

Frequently Asked Questions (FAQ)

As one of the most widely used accounting software solutions, QuickBooks is trusted by millions of businesses for managing finances and streamlining operations. However, with so many features and capabilities, it's common for new and experienced users alike to have questions. In this section, we address some of the most frequently asked questions (FAQs), offer tips for maximizing efficiency, and provide resources to help you continue learning and improving your QuickBooks skills.

Addressing Common Concerns

1. What is the Difference Between QuickBooks Online and QuickBooks Desktop?

QuickBooks Online and **QuickBooks Desktop** are two versions of the software that cater to different business needs. While both can handle similar accounting tasks, they vary in their functionalities, accessibility, and overall experience.

- **QuickBooks Online**:
    - Cloud-based, accessible from anywhere with an internet connection.
    - More suitable for businesses with remote teams or multiple users.
    - Offers automatic software updates and is more flexible in integrating with third-party applications.
    - Offers a mobile app for on-the-go access.
- **QuickBooks Desktop**:

- o Installed software that can only be used on a specific computer unless connected to a server.
- o More customizable with industry-specific versions for specialized businesses.
- o Does not offer real-time syncing or cloud access unless additional services are purchased (e.g., QuickBooks Desktop Cloud Hosting).
- o Typically preferred by businesses that require robust, offline data handling and more complex accounting features.

Choosing between the two depends on your business's specific needs, such as the number of users, the need for mobility, and customization requirements.

---

2. How Do I Set Up QuickBooks for My Business?

Setting up QuickBooks for your business involves several steps, but the process is relatively straightforward.

- **Step 1: Choose Your QuickBooks Version** – Decide whether you will use QuickBooks Online or QuickBooks Desktop based on your business needs.
- **Step 2: Create Your Company File** – Once installed or logged in, create a company file by entering your business information, such as business name, address, tax ID, and industry type.
- **Step 3: Set Up Your Chart of Accounts** – Customize your chart of accounts based on the financial needs of your business. QuickBooks provides a default setup, but you can modify it according to your specific operations.
- **Step 4: Link Your Bank Accounts** – Connect your business bank and credit card accounts to QuickBooks to allow automatic downloading of transactions and easier reconciliation.

- **Step 5**: **Input Opening Balances** – If you're transitioning from another accounting system, input your opening balances as of the date you start using QuickBooks.
- **Step 6**: **Customize Preferences** – Tailor QuickBooks settings for your business, including how you handle invoices, taxes, and payroll.

The setup process in QuickBooks is intuitive, and you can always rely on the in-app guidance or support to assist with any questions during the process.

---

3. How Do I Reconcile My Bank Accounts in QuickBooks?

Bank reconciliation ensures that the transactions in QuickBooks match your actual bank statement. Here's how to reconcile accounts:

- **Step 1**: Go to the **Banking** tab and select **Reconcile**.

- **Step 2**: Choose the account you want to reconcile (e.g., Checking, Credit Card).
- **Step 3**: Enter the statement date and ending balance as shown on your bank statement.
- **Step 4**: Match the transactions in QuickBooks with those on your bank statement. QuickBooks will automatically highlight matching transactions, but you can manually match any unmatched ones.
- **Step 5**: When the difference between QuickBooks and your bank statement is zero, click **Reconcile Now**.

Reconciliation should be done on a monthly basis to ensure that your books are accurate and up-to-date.

---

4. How Can I Automate My Invoice Creation in QuickBooks?

QuickBooks offers a feature called **Recurring Transactions**, which can automate the creation of invoices, bills, and other transactions.

- **Step 1**: Go to **Lists** and select **Recurring Transactions**.
- **Step 2**: Click **New**, then choose the type of transaction (Invoice, Bill, etc.).
- **Step 3**: Set the frequency for the recurring invoice (daily, weekly, monthly).
- **Step 4**: Enter all the necessary details, including customer information, products/services, and amounts.
- **Step 5**: Click **OK** to save, and QuickBooks will automatically generate the invoice according to the selected schedule.

Recurring invoices can be especially helpful for businesses that offer subscription services or have regular, predictable billing cycles.

5. How Do I Add and Manage Multiple Users in QuickBooks?

Managing multiple users in QuickBooks allows for better collaboration and ensures that various members of your team can access the software while maintaining control over sensitive information.

- **Step 1**: Go to the **Company** menu and select **Set Up Users and Passwords**.
- **Step 2**: Click **Set Up Users** and choose the user type (Standard, Admin, etc.).
- **Step 3**: Define the permissions for each user, including which areas of QuickBooks they can access and modify.
- **Step 4**: Enter the user's name and email address and assign them a unique password.
- **Step 5**: Save the settings.

You can add as many users as your subscription allows and set specific permissions to control access to sensitive information, such as payroll data or financial reports.

Tips for Maximizing Efficiency

QuickBooks is a powerful tool, but using it effectively requires some best practices and a few tricks up your sleeve. Here are some tips to help you maximize your efficiency and make the most of QuickBooks:

1. Use Keyboard Shortcuts

QuickBooks offers several keyboard shortcuts that can speed up your workflow, such as:

- **Ctrl + I**: Create an invoice.
- **Ctrl + W**: Write a check.
- **Ctrl + T**: Open the transaction history.
- **Ctrl + E**: Edit a transaction.

These shortcuts help you navigate the software faster without needing to click through multiple menus.

2. Utilize Recurring Transactions and Bank Feeds

As mentioned earlier, setting up recurring transactions for regular invoices, bills, and journal entries saves significant time. Similarly, linking your bank accounts to QuickBooks ensures that transactions are automatically imported, reducing manual data entry.

3. Customize Reports for Easy Access

QuickBooks allows you to customize reports to show the most relevant data for your business. Save these customized reports for quick access, and automate the scheduling of reports for regular email delivery.

4. Regular Reconciliation

Make it a habit to reconcile your bank and credit card accounts regularly. This ensures that your data remains accurate and up-to-date, and helps you identify errors early.

Key Resources for Learning More

To further improve your knowledge and expertise with QuickBooks, there are several resources available to guide you:

1. QuickBooks Help Center (Online)

QuickBooks has an extensive **Help Center** that provides detailed articles, step-by-step guides, and troubleshooting tips. You can search for answers by topic or issue.

2. QuickBooks Tutorials and Webinars

Intuit, the maker of QuickBooks, offers free **tutorials** and **webinars** that cover everything from basic functions to advanced features. These resources are available on the official QuickBooks website and YouTube channel.

3. QuickBooks Community Forum

The **QuickBooks Community** is a forum where users can ask questions, share tips, and learn from each other. It's a great place to connect with other users and get answers from experts.

4. QuickBooks ProAdvisor Program

If you're looking for expert guidance or need a professional to help set up or troubleshoot QuickBooks, the **ProAdvisor** program connects you with certified QuickBooks experts who can provide consulting services and training.

5. Online QuickBooks Courses

There are several online platforms like **Udemy**, **LinkedIn Learning**, and **Coursera** that offer in-depth QuickBooks courses. These can be a great way to learn QuickBooks at your own pace.

6. QuickBooks Blog

QuickBooks has a regularly updated **blog** that covers product updates, best practices, tips, and industry news. It's a useful resource for staying up to date with the latest features and improvements.

Glossary of QuickBooks Terms

A

- **Accounts Payable (AP)**: Money that a business owes to vendors or suppliers for goods or services received but not yet paid for. It is considered a liability on the balance sheet.

- **Accounts Receivable (AR)**: Money that a business is owed by customers for products or services provided on credit. It is an asset on the balance sheet.

- **Account Type**: Defines the nature of the account in QuickBooks, such as Asset, Liability, Income, Expense, or Equity.

- **Adjusting Entries**: Entries made at the end of an accounting period to correct errors or update accounts before financial statements are prepared.

- **Amortization**: The gradual reduction of an intangible asset's value over time, often in the form of a set schedule.

B

- **Balance Sheet**: A financial statement that shows a company's assets, liabilities, and equity at a specific point in time.

- **Bank Reconciliation**: The process of matching the balances in your QuickBooks account to those on your bank statement to ensure consistency.

- **Bill**: A document that records an amount owed to a vendor for goods or services, often used in accounts payable.

- **Billing Rate**: The price charged to a client for services, typically used in project-based billing or hourly work.

- **Budget**: A financial plan that estimates income and expenses for a set period.

- **Business Use Percentage**: A calculation used to determine the percentage of a vehicle, home, or other asset used for business purposes versus personal use, useful for tax deductions.

C

- **Cash Flow**: The movement of money into and out of a business, reflecting the company's liquidity and ability to cover its expenses.

- **Chart of Accounts**: A list of all accounts used by a business to record financial transactions. Accounts are categorized into Assets, Liabilities, Income, Expenses, and Equity.

- **Closing the Books**: The process of finalizing all accounting entries for a particular period, making the financial records ready for the next period.

- **Customer**: A person or organization that purchases goods or services from a business.

- **Credit Memo**: A document issued to a customer to reduce the amount owed on

an invoice, often used in the case of
returns or overpayments.

- **Current Assets**: Assets that are expected
  to be converted into cash or used up
  within one year, such as accounts
  receivable and inventory.

D

- **Data Import**: The process of transferring
  data from one system to another, such as
  importing financial records into
  QuickBooks.

- **Depreciation**: The process of allocating
  the cost of a tangible asset over its useful
  life, reflecting a reduction in its value.

- **Discount**: A reduction in price, often
  given to customers for early payment or

bulk purchases.

- **Draw**: Money taken from the business by the owner, usually a sole proprietor or partner, which is not considered a salary but a distribution of profit.

E

- **Employee**: A person hired by a business to perform specific duties in exchange for wages or salary.

- **Equity**: The owner's share of the business, calculated as the difference between assets and liabilities. It represents the business's net worth.

- **Estimate**: An informal document or quote given to a customer, showing an approximation of the costs for goods or services to be provided.

- **Expense**: The cost of goods or services used by a business to generate revenue, such as rent, utilities, or salaries.

F

- **Financial Statements**: Reports that summarize the financial status of a business, including the balance sheet, income statement, and cash flow statement.

- **Fixed Assets**: Long-term tangible assets like equipment, property, or vehicles, that are used in the operation of a business.

- **Freelancer**: A self-employed individual offering services to clients on a contract basis.

G

- **General Ledger**: A complete record of all financial transactions for a business. The general ledger is used to create financial statements.

- **Gross Profit**: The difference between total sales and the cost of goods sold (COGS), showing the amount of money a company makes from its core business activities before operating expenses.

I

- **Income**: The money earned by a business from selling goods or services, which is recorded on the income statement.

- **Invoice**: A document that requests payment for goods or services rendered, often including details such as the date, items or services, quantity, and price.

- **Inventory**: Goods and materials held by a business for sale or use in its operations, including raw materials, finished goods, and work-in-progress.

- **Interest**: The cost of borrowing money, usually calculated as a percentage of the principal amount.

J

- **Journal Entry**: A record of a transaction in the general ledger, typically consisting of debits and credits to balance the books.

- **Job Costing**: The practice of tracking the expenses associated with specific projects or jobs, often used in industries like construction and consulting.

L

- **Liabilities**: Amounts owed by a business to other parties, such as loans, bills, or accounts payable.

- **Liability Accounts**: Accounts used to track amounts that the business owes, including accounts payable, loans, and credit card balances.

- **Long-Term Liabilities**: Debts that are due more than one year from the balance sheet date, such as long-term loans or mortgages.

M

- **Memorized Transaction**: A saved template for recurring transactions, such as monthly bills or invoices, that QuickBooks can automatically generate.

- **Margin**: The difference between the cost of goods sold and the selling price, expressed as a percentage of the selling price.

- **Mileage Tracking**: A feature in QuickBooks that allows users to track and log business-related vehicle mileage for expense reporting and tax deductions.

N

- **Net Profit**: The amount of profit remaining after all expenses, taxes, and costs have been subtracted from revenue.

- **Nonprofit**: An organization that operates for purposes other than making a profit, typically for charitable, educational, or social purposes.

O

- **Opening Balance**: The initial balance in an account when setting up QuickBooks or transferring from another system.

- **Operating Expenses**: Expenses that are necessary for the day-to-day functioning of the business, excluding the cost of goods sold, such as rent, utilities, and payroll.

P

- **Payroll**: The process of calculating and distributing employee wages, taxes, and deductions.

- **Petty Cash**: A small amount of cash kept on hand for minor business expenses, like office supplies or incidentals.

- **Posting**: The act of transferring journal entries to the general ledger.

- **Profit and Loss Statement (P&L)**: A financial statement that summarizes the revenues, costs, and expenses over a specific period to show the net profit or loss.

- **Purchase Order (PO)**: A document used to authorize a purchase from a vendor. It includes details like quantity, price, and delivery date.

Q

- **QuickBooks Online**: A cloud-based version of QuickBooks that allows for remote access and collaboration.

- **QuickBooks Desktop**: A locally installed version of QuickBooks that is typically used for businesses that require more advanced or industry-specific features.

R

- **Reconciliation**: The process of matching the transactions recorded in QuickBooks with your bank statements to ensure accuracy.

- **Recurring Transactions**: Transactions that repeat on a regular basis, such as monthly bills or invoices, which can be automated in QuickBooks.

- **Receipts**: Proof of payment for goods or services, which can be recorded in QuickBooks to track expenses.

- **Retained Earnings**: The cumulative amount of net income that has been retained in the business, rather than paid out to shareholders or owners.

S

- **Sales Tax**: A tax imposed by the government on the sale of goods or services, which businesses must collect from customers and remit to tax authorities.

- **Self-Employed**: An individual who works for themselves rather than for an employer.

- **Statement of Cash Flows**: A financial statement that shows the movement of cash within the business over a specific period, including cash from operating, investing, and financing activities.

- **Subsidiary Account**: A sub-account within a larger account that provides more detail, such as a customer or vendor account under accounts receivable or payable.

T

- **Trial Balance**: A report that lists all the accounts in the general ledger and their balances, used to check that debits and credits are in balance.

- **Transaction**: Any financial activity that is recorded in QuickBooks, such as sales, purchases, payments, or deposits.

- **Turnover**: The total revenue or sales generated by a business over a specific period.

U

- **Undeposited Funds**: A temporary account in QuickBooks that holds payments received but not yet deposited into a bank account.

V

- **Vendor**: A supplier or provider of goods or services to a business.

- **Vendor Credit**: A reduction in the amount owed to a vendor, typically resulting from a return or overpayment.

W

- **Write-Off**: The act of declaring an asset or account as uncollectible, typically used for bad debts.

- **Wages**: The compensation paid to employees for work performed, typically calculated by the hour, day, or piece.

X

- **Xero**: A competitor to QuickBooks, offering cloud-based accounting software.

Y

- **Year-End Closing**: The process of finalizing all accounts at the end of the fiscal year and preparing for the next period, including generating financial statements and tax reports.

Z

- **Zero Balance**: A situation in which an account has no remaining balance, such as a cleared bank account or fully paid invoice.

Ultimate QuickBooks Bible